Out on Bail

The Crimes of Ireland's Bail Breakers

Out on Bail

The Crimes of Ireland's Bail Breakers

Emer Connolly

Gill & Macmillan

Gill & Macmillan Ltd
Hume Avenue, Park West, Dublin 12
with associated companies throughout the world
www.gillmacmillan.ie

© Emer Connolly 2011
978 0 7171 4816 5

Typography design by Make Communication
Print origination by TypeIT, Dublin
Printed in Sweden by ScandBook AB

This book is typeset in Minion 11.5pt on 14.5pt.

The paper used in this book comes from the wood pulp of
managed forests. For every tree felled, at least one tree is
planted, thereby renewing natural resources.

A CIP catalogue record for this book is available from the
British Library.

5 4 3 2 1

Cover image: The convicted criminal who appears on the front
cover of this book does not feature in any of the cases covered
in *Out on Bail*. The cover image was chosen because it
demonstrates a contempt towards the Irish justice system, an
attitude that is all too common in the country's courts.

Contents

Acknowledgments

I would like to thank every single person who helped me — both professionally and personally — during my research for and writing of this book; to those named in the text and also to the many people who chose to remain anonymous. Thank you to Fergal Tobin and the team at Gill & Macmillan, including Deirdre Rennison Kunz, Teresa Daly, Ciara O'Connor and Jen Patton, whose guidance and support during this project was fantastic. Particular thanks to my editor, Alison Walsh, for her patience and professionalism.

As part of my research for the chapter entitled 'The Good Samaritan', I spoke at length with Tony Dennehy. Tony's brother Finbar was murdered in September 2007. Tony was most generous with his time and spoke openly about his cherished memories of his brother. Sadly, Tony passed away in February 2011. May he Rest In Peace.

Introduction

On Saint Stephen's night 2009, a young schoolteacher was enjoying a night out with friends in Ennis, Co. Clare. Brian Casey, a 26-year-old man from Lissycasey, looked on as a street row broke out between some of his friends and another group. The skirmish was defused within minutes and order was restored. Then, as Brian stood quietly, with his hands in his pockets, he was attacked. He was punched once in the face and was caught off-guard. The severity of the blow caused him to immediately fall to the ground. As he fell backwards, he hit his head off the ground. While on the ground, Brian was punched repeatedly in the face and head. He was taken to hospital, where he died two days later, having suffered a severe head injury and having sustained a skull fracture.

Brian Casey's attackers were Harry Dinan (then aged 29) and his then-22-year-old nephew, Kevin Dinan. Both had several previous convictions. Harry Dinan — who threw the initial punch — was on temporary release at the time of the attack, having received a four-month sentence for road traffic offences in October 2009. Kevin Dinan — who struck the victim as he lay on the ground — was on bail at the time of this offence, having pleaded guilty to burglary and handling stolen property at Ennis Circuit Court five months earlier.

The Dinans later pleaded guilty to manslaughter and were handed jail sentences: Harry of five years and Kevin four years. At their sentencing hearing in November 2010, the judge at Ennis Circuit Court said Mr Casey's death had been 'completely unnecessary'. Brian Casey was entirely blameless and was merely an innocent bystander that night.

This case happened in one corner of the country, but tragically, countless other cases are presented before judges in courts throughout the country every week. While the circumstances surrounding each case are unique, the tragic consequences are the same for the grieving relatives.

In my work as a journalist, I regularly come across cases where crimes have been committed by people on bail, on temporary release or on early release. There are thousands of such cases every year, from minor offences, including public order and criminal damage, to more serious offences, ranging from possession of knives, drug dealing and cases of a sexual nature, to manslaughter and murder. Several issues are of concern to families of victims of crimes committed by people on bail and this book will focus on the human tragedy at the centre of some of these cases.

———

Bail is a bond entered into by an accused person, to ensure that he or she will appear in court to face trial. After an individual is charged with an alleged offence, he or she is either granted bail or remanded in custody. When a person is initially charged with an offence, a decision on whether bail is granted is made by a garda sergeant or member in charge at the garda station where the individual is detained. This decision remains in place until the individual is brought before the district court. At this stage, it is the presiding judge who rules on whether bail is granted or refused, before a trial or sentence. This is made following submissions on behalf of the prosecution (a garda) and the defence (a solicitor). A judge has several factors to take into account, based on the submissions made before the court. Potentially, a decision has consequences for not only a defendant, but society as a whole. Conditions, including a curfew, a requirement to sign on at a garda station, an order to refrain from alcohol and a direction restricting an accused from going near various geographical areas or named individuals, are regularly attached to bail. Rulings made in relation to bail in the district court can be appealed to the High Court.

The Bail Act of 1997 states that a court can, in deciding whether to award or decline bail, take into consideration the nature and degree of seriousness of the alleged offence; the nature and strength of the evidence in support of the charge; any conviction of an accused person for an offence committed while on bail; any previous convictions of the accused and any charges the accused was facing at the time. Having heard evidence on any of those matters, a court can then refuse bail. A refusal is confined to offences of a serious nature, including murder, manslaughter, kidnapping, false imprisonment, rape and sexual offences, serious assaults, drug offences, robberies and burglaries. This legislation also contains new provisions relating to amounts of cash or security to be lodged as part of bail, including conditions relating to good behaviour and allowing forfeiture of bail where the conditions are breached.

In 2007, the Bail Act was amended, to include changes, one of which allows a chief superintendent of An Garda Síochána to go to court and object to bail. This objection would be on the grounds that it is necessary to detain someone either to protect witnesses from intimidation, or to prevent further crime being committed.

However, despite the tightening of the bail laws, figures have shown that the number of serious offences being committed by people out on bail has risen consistently over the years and, at the same time, the prisons remain overcrowded. In 1992, the number of crimes committed by people on bail stood at 2,791. This increased to 5,440 crimes in 1995. The figure had dramatically increased by 2009, when there were 27,228 offences recorded where the suspected offender was on bail. While this was a decrease of eight per cent on the figure for 2008, nevertheless, it is a startling statistic.

The types of crimes committed by those out on bail vary from assault, possession of a firearm, burglary, to drugs offences, but figures show that some very serious crimes are being committed by people out on bail and the level of seriousness of some of the offences is alarming. Take for example, murder. In 2007, there were 14 murders in Ireland where the chief suspect was out on bail. There were eight in 2008 and five in 2009. In 2007, there were 31 murder threats committed by people out on bail. There were 35 in 2008 and 28 in 2009. Furthermore, in 2007, 18 sexual offences were committed by people on bail, 26 offences in 2008 and 14 in 2009. Rape and sexual offences are particularly distressing for the victims and knowing that the perpetrator was out on bail when the crime was committed undoubtedly adds to the pain. In May 2010, it emerged that 15 murders had been committed where the chief suspect was out on bail, between the start of 2008 and March 2010. According to figures from the Central Statistics Office (cso), the chief suspects in thousands of other serious crimes were on bail during that same time frame. This included 47 sexual offences, 70 murder threats, 508 robberies from the person and 122 aggravated burglaries.

This revelation prompted Fine Gael to suggest that the figures showed the bail laws are not working. The party's then justice spokesman, Charlie Flanagan, speaking in May 2010, said that, in reality, people released on bail are going to continue to commit serious crimes. 'Put simply, Ireland's bail law is not protecting Irish citizens. Dangerous criminals under investigation are being re-released into society and in some cases go on to kill people. Unless the standard is raised in regard to who is let out on bail, the level of bail crime will continue to tear at the fabric of our communities.' However, Justice Minister Dermot Ahern (Fianna Fáil) told the Dáil at that time that the government cannot restrict bail conditions much further, or it would contravene the personal freedom provisions of the

Constitution and of the European Convention on Human Rights. 'We are trying to tighten up a number of issues, bring in new conditions and lower the bar in relation to seriousness of offences, where there would be a more strict criteria on the granting of bail,' said Mr Ahern.

One of the key reforms recommended by Fine Gael is a radical overhaul of the bail laws, with a view to reducing the number of offences committed by those released on bail. It has also proposed that measures be introduced to allow those on bail to be electronically tagged. The party believes that electronic tagging should be used for prisoners on temporary release. Fine Gael proposed a Victims Rights Bill in 2008, which would give new rights to victims of crime. One of the proposals it contained was that victims would have a say in bail applications and applications for early release and parole by offenders. However, this Bill was rejected in the Dáil.

Sinn Féin has expressed the view that lengthy delays in the justice system are problematic and believes that everyone arrested or detained should be entitled to a trial within a reasonable time, or, to release pending trial. Its submission, 'Policing with the Community in 2009' recommends that the annual garda policing plan should include targets and performance indicators aimed at reducing any delays that may contribute to the length of time spent on bail. Speaking during a Dáil debate in 2008, the party's justice spokesman, Deputy Aengus Ó Snodaigh said: 'There is justifiable public anger at the volume of crimes being committed while on bail . . . resourcing the justice system including the courts, the DPP and free legal aid so that justice can be administered promptly would put the judiciary in a better position to make the most appropriate decision on bail applications. In addition, by decreasing the length of time spent on bail, the number of offences committed would be reduced. Judicial guidelines governing decision-making on bail applications should be produced.'

Sinn Féin's position is that a person is innocent until proven guilty and the right to bail should be protected. However, it recognises that the right to bail is not unlimited in that bail can be refused where an individual is a genuine flight risk or who poses a risk of interfering with witnesses. According to the party's justice policy: 'Sinn Féin recognises that the granting of bail to detained persons, particularly when the offence is for a violent/sexual offence, can be problematic for the victims of such crimes, and we believe that judges should take these concerns into account when setting bail conditions. However, the presumption in favour of bail is a fundamental human right and is protected by Article 5(3) of the European Convention on Human Rights.'

The Labour Party has also proposed measures in relation to the granting of bail. In its 2007 general election manifesto, the party proposed that a full-time court of criminal appeal be established and that it be afforded the opportunity to hear appeals in bail cases. It has also suggested that bail supervision and support schemes be introduced, in an effort to avoid children committing crimes on bail. The party says that going forward, it will consider further developing its policies in relation to bail.

In the meantime, victim support groups have expressed their concern at the alarmingly high rates of offences. Over the years, there have been repeated calls for a root-and-branch review of bail laws and practices. Advic (Advocates for Victims of Homicide) has called for laws to be introduced to prevent people accused of murder being granted bail before their trials. Advic founder member, Joan Deane has addressed the bail issue from the point of view of the victims and said that the Irish people have been let down by the interpretation and application of the country's bail laws. She has called for the system to be re-balanced, to take into account the rights of victims. 'In the interest of fairness and balance, if a jury has to be informed of the good character of an accused, is it not reasonable to expect that they also be informed, before retiring to deliberate, when an accused has prior pertinent convictions, for example, for violent assault, or was out on bail for such when the crime took place?' she asked.

Another cause of anxiety for victims of crime and their families is the issue of temporary release. Many of them don't understand the meaning of temporary or early release and cannot understand why a ten-year sentence doesn't mean ten years spent in prison. They are also concerned that those on temporary release are not adequately monitored. Many are also unaware that the majority of prisoners are entitled to statutory remission of a quarter of their sentences. There is also a discretionary granting of additional remission of up to one third, where a prisoner has shown good conduct while in prison and where his behaviour has led the authorities to believe he is not likely to re-offend. This is only given in exceptional cases and is approved by the Minister for Justice.

Life-sentence prisoners — including several of those featured in this book — are generally invited to apply to the Parole Board for parole, after they have served seven years of their sentence. Recent statistics suggest that 'model prisoners' serving life sentences will not be recommended for supervised release until they have served around 18 years. However, each case is different and there are more than a dozen life-sentence prisoners who have already served over 25 years in prison custody.

The Parole Board's Annual Report (2008) says that the cases of 66 prisoners were referred to the Board for review during that year. This was compared to 74 in 2007. In 2008, the Board made recommendations to the Minister for Justice, Equality and Law Reform in 67 cases. The recommendations in 62 cases were accepted by the Minister, who ultimately decides on a prisoner's fate. The Minister did not make a decision in three of those cases as the release of the prisoners on remission was imminent. In two other cases, the Minister did not agree with the recommendations of the Board.

When formulating its recommendations, the Board states

that it is primarily concerned with the risk to members of the community, which the release of a life-sentence prisoner or the early release of a determinate-sentence prisoner would pose.

Temporary-release arrangements operate similarly to a system of parole, which is a feature of prison systems worldwide. According to the Prison Service, 'Each case is examined on its own merits and the safety of the public is paramount when decisions are made. In addition, all releases are subject to conditions, which in the vast majority of cases include a requirement to report on a regular basis to the offender's garda station. Of course, any offender who breaches his or her conditions may be arrested and returned to prison immediately by the gardaí.

'Candidates for temporary release are identified by a number of different means. These include the recommendation of the Prison Governor or the therapeutic services in the prisons ... It is very important to note that it does not necessarily follow that a prisoner will receive temporary release even if the recommendation is to that effect. The periods of temporary release granted can vary greatly from a few hours following a family bereavement to, for example, a requirement to report to the prison every twelve months in the case of a life-sentence prisoner who has been released into the community a considerable time ago,' said a spokesman for the Prison Service.

According to the Prison Service, the average number of prisoners on temporary release at any one time in 2009 was 535, of the total number of 3,881 prisoners in the system. In 2008, there was an average of 273 prisoners on temporary release at any one time during the year, out of 3,544 prisoners in total. In 2007, the figure was 157 prisoners on temporary release, out of 3,321 prisoners in the system, while the figure in 2006 was 146 out of a total of 3,191 prisoners.

The figures are an indication of the overcrowding issue in the country's prisons. For example, on 21 May 2010, there were 917 prisoners on temporary release from prison. On the same day, there were 4,276 prisoners in custody, against a bed capacity of 4,066, according to figures obtained from the Prison Service press office.

The figures for April 2010 for those granted weekly reviewable temporary release indicate that an average of 36 prisoners were granted temporary release per day (836 prisoners during the month, on average) which is 0.86 per cent of the average number in custody in April (4,100 prisoners). The average daily number of people on temporary release for the month of April was 836 people, which represents approximately 16.3 per cent of the total number of prisoners in the system. Given the strong link between the country's bail laws and the prison system, the creation of more prison spaces is essential if the issue of re-offending on bail is to be seriously addressed.

I have chosen ten cases in this book, where serious crimes have been committed by people out on bail, on temporary release or on early release. I have also focused on one case where the defendant breached his bail and disappeared after committing an offence which resulted in the loss of two young lives. The actions of David Naughton, who was charged in connection with a fatal road accident, had a profound effect on the families of the young girls killed, who waited every day for justice. Naughton was eventually re-arrested and was jailed for dangerous driving, causing the deaths of Lorna Mahoney and Stacey Haugh, in west Clare in 2003.

Eight of the eleven cases featured in this book resulted in loss of life; one focuses on a vicious rape by a man who was on bail at the time; another focuses on a drug dealer who offended while on bail in Cork; while another features a man who broke into the homes of several elderly citizens while he was on early release from prison.

Swiss couple Hans-Peter and Arlette Riedo will never get over the loss of their daughter, Manuela. The 17-year-old was murdered while on a visit to Galway in 2007. Her killer, Gerald Barry, was on bail at the time. Another young woman whose life was needlessly taken was Sylvia Roche-Kelly. She was out celebrating her 33rd birthday in Limerick in 2007 when she met a man who would later murder her in a hotel bedroom they shared that night. It was a chance encounter, but would lead to her brutal death. Sylvia's killer, Jerry McGrath, was on bail at the time for an assault on a female taxi driver.

Another case that captured the hearts of the people of Ireland was that of retired schoolteacher Nancy Nolan. The 80-year-old was murdered in her Co. Galway home on Valentine's Day 2000. Her killer was Thomas Murray, who was on day release from prison, where he was serving a life sentence for another murder committed 19 years earlier.

Another innocent life stolen was that of Brian Mulvaney, a Dublin teenager who was attacked by a group of young men in Dublin in March 2000. One of them, Brian Willoughby, who was later convicted of his murder, was on bail at the time in connection with other violent incidents.

Three years before Brian Mulvaney's murder, another Dublin couple had all their hopes and dreams for their son suddenly dashed when he was stabbed to death just a stone's throw from his home. Marc O'Keeffe was just 20 when he was killed by Michael Doyle, in May 1997. Doyle, who was later convicted of the manslaughter of Marc, was on bail in connection with a violent assault on a taxi driver at the time of the killing.

Two other men who died in horrendous circumstances were Noel Carmody and Finbar Dennehy. Noel Carmody, a teacher, was beaten to death in Limerick in 2003 by two men, one who was on bail and the other who was unlawfully at large, having failed to return to jail after temporary release. Finbar Dennehy was murdered in his Dublin home in 2007 by a man to whom he kindly offered a place to stay. A bench warrant had been issued for his killer, Michael Downes, eight months earlier, after he failed to appear in court.

All of these cases raise disturbing questions and there are painful memories for the victims' families. The bail laws are the subject of much debate in Ireland, but it is the human tragedy that makes the issue so real.

Chapter 1
'Our Angel'

She was their only child; their pride and joy. She was vivacious, energetic, bright and bubbly. Her proud parents looked forward to her going to college and fulfilling her dreams of a career in hotel management. They anticipated the day their 'angel' would get married and have children. But those dreams would never become a reality, as their little girl was taken from them in shocking circumstances, more than a thousand miles from their Swiss home.

Hans-Peter and Arlette Riedo's dreams for their daughter were torn to shreds on an autumn evening in Galway city, when she was violently murdered. Seventeen-year-old Manuela had her parents' blessing when she chose to go to Galway to learn English for two weeks. It was her first time away on her own. Manuela arrived, with her class, in Galway on Saturday 6 October 2007. Two days later, she was murdered. Her body was discovered on waste ground near Lough Atalia in Renmore, on the outskirts of Galway city, on Tuesday morning, 9 October 2007. She had died from asphyxia, due to neck compression.

Her killer was a local man named Gerald Barry, then aged 27, of Rosán Glas, Rahoon, Galway and originally from nearby

Mervue. At the time, the father-of-two was out on bail for an alleged assault on his ex-partner two months earlier. He was charged with assaulting his ex-partner on 16 August 2007, and within days he appeared before a sitting of Galway District Court, where he was granted bail. Barry had raped a French student on 16 August 2007, but had not been charged in relation to that offence at the time he killed Manuela. In April 2008, he was charged with raping the French student. He pleaded guilty in May 2009 and was later handed two life sentences.

Manuela's killing sent shock waves through the community in Galway city. The discovery of Manuela's body led to a major garda investigation being launched. A thorough search of the scene where her body was found was carried out, as the area was combed for every possible clue, while underwater divers carried out searches in Lough Atalia. Forensic tests were carried out on items of clothing seized during the investigation. Detectives from the highly skilled unit, the National Bureau of Criminal Investigation, were drafted in to help with the investigation.

Gerald Barry was arrested in connection with the death of Manuela Riedo on 18 October 2007. The following day, he was charged with her murder and was brought before Galway District Court. He was jeered by locals as he was escorted into the court, as onlookers expressed howls of outrage at the killing of the young woman. Barry was remanded in custody to Castlerea Prison in Co. Roscommon, to appear again in court a week later. The Book of Evidence was served on 31 March 2008, and he was returned for trial — in custody — to the Central Criminal Court.

Barry went on trial at the Central Criminal Court in March 2009, accused of murdering Manuela on 8 October 2007. Barry, who was then aged 28, pleaded not guilty to the murder, but admitted stealing her camera and mobile phone on the same date. At the end of his trial, he was found guilty by a jury of murdering Manuela and was jailed for life.

Manuela was one of 43 students from Freiburg School in

Switzerland who travelled to Galway to learn English. It was part of an annual two-week trip undertaken by the school to Galway, where accommodation had been arranged for the students and their teachers. They were enrolled in language schools in Galway city and allocated to different host families. The group had been due to return home to Switzerland on 20 October 2007. Manuela was staying with a host family in Renmore Park in Galway city. She was part of a group that met at Eyre Square, in the heart of Galway City Centre, on Sunday afternoon, 7 October, and in the King's Head pub on High Street in the city centre later that evening.

On the evening of Monday, 8 October, Manuela returned to her host family for dinner at around 5.30 p.m. She left there between 7 p.m. and 8 p.m. to go into the city centre, where she was due to meet friends. It later emerged that she and a friend had found a short cut to the city, by the railway line, and had walked that route together prior to that Monday night. Manuela walked the path, known locally as 'The Line', alone on the evening of 8 October, on her way to meet her friends in the King's Head pub. She never arrived.

Friends raised the alarm after she failed to attend class the following day, Tuesday 9 October, and they were unable to contact her. Gardaí were alerted. At around 9.15 a.m. on Tuesday 9 October, a man walking to work made a shocking discovery. He found the body of a young woman near Lough Atalia in Renmore, a half mile from where Manuela was staying. The body was naked from the waist down. Clothing and a bag, belonging to Manuela, were found nearby. The body was later identified as that of Manuela.

State Pathologist Professor Marie Cassidy told Gerald Barry's murder trial at the Central Criminal Court in March 2009 that Manuela died from strangulation and had also sustained head injuries. It was possible, she said, that the young woman had lost consciousness due to an assault, before she died from asphyxia. The jury was told that Manuela had sustained an

'unusual' injury, in that a piece of skin had been removed —
with a sharp object — from the groin area. When her body was
found, she was naked from the waist down, partially covered by
her coat, which had been secured by a rock. Professor Cassidy
told the jury that the teenager's neck had been compressed, due
to contact. She said that death could have been due to asphyxia,
as a result of neck compression. There was a bump and
laceration on the back of Manuela's head, possibly caused by
her head being struck or having struck a surface.

The trial heard that phone calls made on Gerald Barry's
mobile phone bounced off a mast in the Lough Atalia area on
the night of Manuela's death. However, he told gardaí he was
not in that area that night. He claimed he had spent the
afternoon and evening with his brother and brother-in-law. He
told gardaí that he was not in Galway city that day or night and
said he did not leave Salthill. The court also heard that Barry
had sold a mobile phone to his sister's boyfriend nine days after
the killing, for €30. The mobile phone had belonged to
Manuela. He said he did this because he wanted money for
drink. Gardaí found Manuela's camera in the accused's
bedroom.

At the trial, it was revealed that Barry's DNA was found in a
condom that had been located at the scene of Manuela's death.
A witness from the forensic science laboratory in Dublin told
the trial that she had examined swabs taken from the accused
and the profile of the condom's contents matched his DNA
profile. She said the chances of a person unrelated to Barry
having the same profile were one in a thousand million. She
also said that she had generated a mixed DNA profile from the
outside of the condom and the profile contained all the
elements of DNA from both the defendant and Manuela.
However, during a garda interview, Barry said he hadn't used a
condom in the previous five years and didn't know how his DNA
came to be on it.

Barry gave evidence at the trial and said Manuela's death was an accident and he had not meant to harm her. He told the court how he met Manuela near a shop in Renmore some time after 7 o'clock on the evening of her death. He said she asked him for the time and she told him she was walking into the city to meet friends. He said he told her there was a quicker way to get there and they walked together. They reached an area where the track leads up to The Line and, he said, they kissed.

'I told her I thought she was beautiful and I leaned in and kissed her. She kissed me back. We were kissing and fondling and a few minutes later I suggested we lie down on the grass. I put my jacket down and she put her jacket down. I suggested we have sex. She asked if I had a condom. I said I did,' he told the court. He said they had sex and then lay on the ground together. Manuela then sat up and said she had to go and meet her friends. Barry said he then grabbed her from behind and asked her to spend some time with him. He said she didn't respond and she slid onto the ground.

'Her head kind of flopped. I shook her and got no response,' he said. Asked if he knew how Manuela had sustained a laceration to the back of her head, he replied, 'I don't know, unless it happened when her head flopped.' He said he then pulled her body to where it was discovered the following morning. Asked in court why he had done this, he said, 'I don't know, to be honest with you.' He said he then placed her jacket over her and put a stone over the jacket, so that it wouldn't come off her body. He then tossed her clothes into the bushes. Her bag hit the ground, causing her camera and phone to fall out. He took the camera and phone, but couldn't explain why he had done this. 'I don't know. It's just something I did,' he told the court. Asked why he had told lies to gardaí after Manuela's death, he replied, 'Because I thought if I kept denying it, it'd just go away.' It was put to him under cross-examination that he attacked and murdered Manuela, to which he replied, 'It was an accident. I didn't mean to cause her any harm.' Asked why he hadn't called the emergency number 999, he said, 'Because she was dead.'

At the end of the seven-day trial, on 21 March 2009, the jury of six men and six women convicted Barry of murder, after deliberating for just over two-and-a-half hours. The trial judge, Mr Justice Barry White, jailed him for life. Barry was also handed a ten-year jail sentence for the theft of Manuela's mobile phone and camera.

But this wasn't Barry's first conviction. He had a long history of violence and a string of previous convictions, including one for violent disorder. This was in connection with the death of a man called Colm Phelan (26) from Roscrea in Co. Tipperary, who died after being hit on the head with a bottle during a violent incident at Eyre Square in Galway city in July 1996. Barry, who was aged 16 at the time of the attack, was sentenced to five years in jail for that offence. He was also handed a two-year jail sentence in 1998 for an assault on an elderly man during a break-in. The victim had sight in only one eye at the time, but lost the sight following the assault. Barry also had previous convictions for possession of drugs, theft, burglary and road traffic offences.

Following the trial into the death of Manuela Riedo, Barry had a number of other court appearances ahead of him. In May 2009, he pleaded guilty to the oral and anal rape of a 21-year-old French student at a sports pitch at Mervue, Galway, in the early hours of 16 August 2007 (less than two months before he murdered Manuela). Like Manuela, the French woman had been walking alone when she encountered Barry. Tragically, both women had come to Ireland to study and both had fallen victim to the same criminal. At the court hearing in connection with the attack on her, the French woman begged the judge not to let Barry out of prison. In her victim impact statement, which was read to the court by a garda, the French student said, 'He is not a human or a man. He is a liar, a rapist and a murderer. I beg you not to let him out, because he will do it again.' She said she thought she was going to die when he attacked her. 'Why was I let go? Why am I still breathing?' she asked. At the sentencing hearing in July 2009, Mr Justice Paul Carney said Barry had a 'propensity to kill and rape' and was highly likely to do so again. The judge handed down two life sentences.

At Galway District Court on 24 March 2010, Barry was handed sentences totalling two years, for a number of offences. He was sentenced to six months in jail for assaulting his former partner and six months for assaulting his then-two-year-old son, in August 2007. He was handed two five-month jail terms for assaulting two gardaí in Galway in March 2007 and a two-month sentence for resisting garda arrest. A two-month sentence, to run concurrently, was imposed for breaching a protection order in the early hours of 16 August 2007. Judge Mary Fahy noted, at that court, that when Barry was brought before a special sitting of the court in August 2007 for the alleged assault on the woman and child, the woman had told a visiting judge who was presiding during the court holiday period that she was not afraid of Barry. Bail had been granted.

––––

There is no doubt but that Gerald Barry's crimes have left an indelible mark on his victims and their families, not least Manuela Riedo's heartbroken parents. Since Manuela's death, the Counselling Centre of Victim Aid (Beratungsstelle Opferhilfe Bern) has provided support for Hans-Peter and Arlette Riedo. At their home in the little village of Hinter-kappelen, 16 kilometres south of Bern, in Switzerland, the couple agreed to talk to me about their daughter's life and cruel death. (They speak German and have very little English, so Susanne Nielen Gangwisch, from the Counselling Centre of Victim Aid, kindly agreed to translate the interview from German to English.)

Their neat home is a shrine to Manuela. From the moment you walk into the small two-bedroomed apartment, everything is focused on Hans-Peter's and Arlette's daughter. Several of Manuela's treasured belongings are sprinkled around her little bedroom; from her clothes, to her music collection, to her concert tickets and postcards, to her toys and ornaments. A jersey from her favourite ice hockey team, Schlittschuh Club Bern, hangs prominently on the wardrobe door, close to a purple top she wore in Galway on the night before she died. They are all reminders of a beautiful young lady, who was so close to her parents' hearts. Her single bed is still neatly made.

It is like any teenage girl's bedroom. The room is as she left it when she departed for Ireland. It is as though her parents are waiting for her to return. Instead, Hans-Peter and Arlette visit her grave every day.

Dozens of photographs of Manuela, at various stages of her short life, fill every prominent space in her parents' apartment. From Manuela as a beaming baby; to Manuela as a bubbly little girl; through to an energetic, radiant Manuela just a day before her brutal murder. In each of those photographs, she is smiling widely. She was a very happy young lady and had so much to offer life. Her mother Arlette deeply treasures ten albums featuring family photographs, including dozens of images of their daughter with family and friends. As she talked about her only daughter, she flicked through the photographs on several occasions, recounting the happy memories attached to each image.

During the course of our interview, Hans-Peter and Arlette reflect on Manuela's short life and while most of the memories are overwhelmingly happy ones, the laughter turns to tears as they talk about her cruel end. They have experienced a huge amount of pain over the past few years, but find that talking about it helps them to cope. The circumstances of Manuela's death continue to pain them immensely and several unanswered questions haunt them. As they talk and share family photographs of Manuela, it is clear that they will never recover from the heartbreak of their daughter being taken away from them so young and so callously. A huge void will always remain in their lives.

Since Manuela's death, Hans-Peter and Arlette have experienced a mixture of good and bad days, but their strength gets them through every day. Sometimes Arlette finds it difficult to sleep at night. Her voice quivers and her eyes fill at the thought of the purgatory she has been forced to face. 'A lot of people ask how can you live with this? How can you manage the daily life? We cannot imagine, but we don't take any medication. We don't want it; we don't need it. We didn't want to have, at any time, psychological support, because in our opinion we are not ill. We are sad and we had this terrible loss but our lives have to go on and not with medication or therapy,' says Arlette.

'We try to do new things. We don't visit places we visited with Manuela, for example, restaurants, or make little trips we did with Manuela. I went skiing with Manuela and have never been skiing since,' says Hans-Peter, adding, 'It doesn't always work. We do new things but there are other things that remind us of Manuela, for example a rainbow.'

Hans-Peter and Arlette had always taken great care of their daughter. Hans-Peter regularly collected Manuela when she was out at night, to ensure that she would arrive home safely. 'Her trip to Ireland was her first trip without us parents. Manuela would have soon turned eighteen and we wanted to gradually let her discover the world on her own. We had heard only good things about Ireland and thus we had no misgivings about sending her to this beautiful country. Before she left, she said that she hoped to get through the two weeks without feeling homesick and that the trip would be a test for future long trips,' says her father.

Manuela was a meticulous individual and prepared well for her trip to Galway. She photocopied recipes from a cookery magazine about popular foods in Ireland, while she wrote lists of the personal belongings she would bring — such as warm clothes, jewellery and her ipod. As soon as each item was packed into her suitcase, she would mark it off her list. 'She informed herself very well before she went to Galway,' beams her proud father.

The closeness Manuela enjoyed with her parents is evident in many ways, one of which was through a note they placed in her suitcase prior to her leaving for Galway. It was a postcard, with the words, 'Dear Manuela. We wish you a nice time in Ireland. In thoughts, we are with you. Papa and Mama'. After her death, the note was found in the room Manuela stayed in in the home of her host family in Galway.

———

As Arlette and Hans-Peter sit down to talk about their daughter, they recall the moment they were alerted to the fact that something was wrong.

'On Tuesday, 9 October, at 4.30 p.m., we received a call from the school in Freiburg here in Switzerland, where Manuela was going to school. The sentence was, "We have a problem with Manuela in Ireland." I asked, "Which kind of problem? Did she forget anything?" They told me that Manuela wasn't at school in the morning in Galway. They asked me if I could imagine that Manuela would depart on her own to Switzerland; did she have any problems? I said, "No, never, ever." If she had any problems, she would contact the teacher,' recalls Arlette.

Her parents were concerned at this stage as Manuela had never missed a day at school. Hans-Peter then telephoned one of the teachers who had travelled to Galway with Manuela's group. The teacher told him he was in the garda station in Galway, where he had been for the previous five hours. 'He informed me that in the media, they have heard that they found a body in the morning, but at that moment they are not informed if it is female or male,' said Hans-Peter, adding, 'The teacher said that he was now ready to see the body for identification but he was not sure if it was Manuela or not, but it didn't look very good.'

Hans-Peter and Arlette experienced a sudden rush of emotions. Shock, horror, alarm and disbelief all mingled together. There were so many questions, but nobody could provide answers. They were severely hampered by the fact that they were hundreds of miles away, while the language barrier didn't help in their efforts to acquire information. They were helpless. Through all of this, Arlette just didn't want to believe that Manuela was dead, while Hans-Peter's gut feeling told him otherwise. 'I didn't want to believe anything,' said Arlette. Hans-Peter added, 'I was sure that it was Manuela. I had sensitive feelings that it was. I thought very logically. I thought if there was some person missing and a body found, that it must be the same, in such a small town like Galway; that it fitted together, body and missing person.'

As the frantic waiting went on, the couple made several telephone calls to people they knew in both Switzerland and Galway, in an effort to establish what was happening. Finally, at 9.30 p.m. that evening, their worst fears were confirmed. Manuela's body had been identified in Galway. Their only daughter was dead.

'A few minutes after the call [from Galway, confirming that Manuela was dead] the doorbell rang and it was the police from this village. There was a letter with information about the death. Only two policemen — no churchmen, for example — had this paper. I had to sign this paper. It was an official document. It was a very cold business. I cried and broke a bottle. I thought it could not be true. I didn't want to believe it. I took a photo and a candle and put it outside the door for the night,' recalls Arlette.

The slow trickle of information over the days that followed

frustrated them and Arlette says they learned of the various bits of information 'piece by piece. It took a long time.' Hans-Peter and Arlette chose to remain at home in Switzerland and didn't visit Galway. One week later, on 16 October, Manuela's body was returned home. Hans-Peter and Arlette met gardaí at Zurich airport and her body was returned to them, along with some of her clothes and other personal belongings that she had brought to Ireland with her.

'In the beginning they wanted to send ashes,' said Hans-Peter, adding, 'But we didn't want this. We wanted the body. We wanted to see the body and the whole family wanted to say "goodbye". It wasn't really Manuela. It wasn't her smile. The face was a little sad.' He continues, 'I had the feeling it wasn't really Manuela. We began to look for what of Manuela was still there. The eyes: no. The eyes were closed. It wasn't the face who lived. The nose had changed. At that moment, I said Manuela had the nose she had always wanted to have, the small little nose.'

'I had the feeling that Manuela wanted to say to us, "Mama and Papa, I felt a lot of pain. I'm so sorry." It was very hard,' adds her mother.

Now, a few years on, Arlette remains frustrated that some of her questions relating to her daughter's death have never been answered. They attended Gerald Barry's trial and hoped that any questions they had would be answered then, but she says this was not the case.

'I cannot understand why they do not respect that some people want to know all the details, for example, the photo of the finding place. I have a feeling that I have to see this photo. Then I can finish this part. But until I have seen this, I cannot finish this part. I want to see this so that I really know where it was, because there are several versions about where it [Manuela's body] was exactly found. It's important for us,' said Arlette.

'One policeman told us the eyes were closed. Another said the eyes were open. There are different versions. We don't know. The photo would show the reality, the truth,' says Hans-Peter.

Arlette adds, 'I asked for this and some personal things for Manuela, a second camera, for example. She had two cameras. No-one said anything about this second camera. I received not the camera but the photos from the camera [in March 2010]. The memory stick, I didn't receive it. Only the photos in an album ... I want to be informed about the whole file and about these criminal things he [Gerald Barry] did before. In the court ... the policeman read this very quickly, all these criminal things, but we want to be informed in more detail.'

As Arlette and Hans-Peter speak little English, they found parts of the trial difficult to follow. They felt that the evidence moved along at a fast pace and they couldn't keep up with it. They found that this was particularly acute when Gerald Barry was giving evidence, as they couldn't understand everything he said. 'Something we missed, for example, was the statement of Gerald Barry in the trial; exactly the words, the document, speaking in the trial and his statement, I missed. We wish to have a written form of the statement,' Arlette says.

'During the trial there was a photo documentation,' she says, referring to the dossier of crime-scene photos distributed in the court at the trial. 'The jury had one, the prosecution had one, the judge and so on, but we didn't. They very often talked about this, page number three, this photo etc. We cannot understand why we cannot get such documentation. It was very frustrating for us. We came to the court to get all this information. We wanted to be informed, but when we arrived back home in Switzerland we had questions that were not answered during the trial. The hope was that the questions would be answered, but it didn't work,' says Arlette.

'We feel we had to answer a lot of questions, give a lot of information to the investigation and on the other side, they don't give these documents,' she adds, her frustration clear.

Hans-Peter agrees. 'If we received something, we had to ask several times for this. Every little information, we had to work hard to get it.'

Arlette is also anxious to see the CCTV footage taken in Galway on the evening before Manuela died, where she and her friend were seen on camera walking along the street. She is also keen to see a photograph of her daughter's body, which was taken in the hospital in Galway, in an effort to understand exactly what happened to her. 'The public view camera in Galway [CCTV] makes a recording of this evening. A friend of Manuela was a witness and she had to watch this recording several times. Now we are ready to watch this recording, too, but it's not possible. I want to see a photo from the body in the hospital. I don't want to *have* it. I would be content to see it. The teachers saw Manuela there and I, as her mother, want to see this photo too. I want to see this so I can see its effect; the reality. Now I have only the fantasy and sometimes it's worse than to see the fact.'

The Riedos do not believe they will ever know the exact truth behind Manuela's killing, as only one person knows this — her killer. 'We believe that we don't know exactly what had happened because only the murderer knows exactly what happened. One question, for example, is from where was this guy coming, from the city side or from the Renmore side? Did Manuela see her murderer or was he behind her? At the trial, he only told his own fantasy version, that he met Manuela and she agreed to sleep with him and such fantasy,' says Arlette.

They don't ever expect to hear the truth behind the circumstances of her death and say they have never received an apology — in person — from Gerald Barry. 'Because of his personality, we didn't expect it and it wouldn't be sincere. There is no sorry for what he has done,' says Hans-Peter. The court process was very difficult for the Riedos because they feel that Barry had a voice at the trial and they didn't. While they believed, deep down, that a guilty verdict would be returned, nevertheless there was always some fear that he may have been acquitted. 'He had more rights than the parents, in general. He had the possibility to prepare himself for the trial. We hadn't.

His statement was the worst thing; his lies. We know they were lies, but it was so hard to hear this about our own daughter, that she agreed to be intimate with him. It was so wrong. He said it was an accident. That was his version. During the sentencing he didn't show any emotions,' says Arlette.

Hans-Peter says that while the outcome of the trial couldn't be predicted, he always believed that the right verdict would be recorded by the jury. 'You never know exactly but with this evidence, we hadn't really doubts about the verdict of guilty. However, in the early time, he always had luck with the justice system,' he says.

As they sat together with grace and dignity during the trial in Dublin, Hans-Peter and Arlette heard that Barry had had issues with alcohol and drug-abuse in the past and that he had a poor upbringing. However, they are refusing to allow this to be used as an excuse for what he did to their daughter. 'It's no excuse. Other people who had [the] same story, same history, don't do such things. It's not really an excuse,' says Arlette. 'Everybody is responsible for their own actions. He had ten years to change his way of life but he doesn't want to do this. He has time enough to think about it now,' says Hans-Peter.

The Riedos are relieved that Barry is now in prison and they live in hope that he will never be released. They say they will never forgive him for the unbearable grief he has put them through. They have visited Ireland several times since Manuela's death and say they will continue to do so, as long as her killer is in prison. They do not bear any ill feelings towards the people of Ireland, from whom they have received fantastic support. It had been suggested that they would take legal action against the Irish State arising from Manuela's death, but they confirm that this will not happen.

'That was mentioned in the Irish media. No, it's not true. The system made a mistake but we do not want to take legal action against the State, no,' says Arlette.

Since Manuela's death, Hans-Peter and Arlette have forged

relationships with several people in Ireland, many of whom they now regard as their friends. They have been in regular contact with the family of Colm Phelan (the man who was killed in Galway in 1996. Gerald Barry was jailed for violent disorder arising out of that attack). They are also keen to meet the French student who Barry raped, weeks before he killed Manuela.

'It could have happened in Switzerland, too. What happened doesn't depend on Ireland,' says Hans-Peter. They believe that an error in the system allowed Barry to be free on the day he killed Manuela. To this day, Manuela's grieving father cannot understand why Barry was granted bail, prior to killing Manuela; given his violent history. 'There are mistakes which happened. Manuela was in the wrong place at the wrong time, but the murder was in a place where he shouldn't have been allowed to be. If the system had worked, he hadn't had the possibility to be there. We blame the justice system for this. If their system had worked, it couldn't have happened. I don't blame Ireland, but the system; not Ireland and the people. It happened in Switzerland several times, such tragic cases and nothing changed. Many people ask us, "Are you angry with Ireland and with the people?" And we say, "No, it's not Ireland, it's the system and the system is the same in Switzerland and it could have happened in Switzerland too",' says Hans-Peter.

'The system isn't so wrong. It works, but they are making mistakes, because if someone does his or her first criminal act, it's ok to be on bail after this, but someone like Gerald Barry, with such a long list of criminal acts, should not be allowed to be on bail. The system doesn't work when they make mistakes. Such an individual shouldn't be set free. How could they give him bail?' he asked.

When the Riedos learned for the first time that their daughter's killer was on bail for another alleged offence at the time of her killing, they found it very difficult to comprehend and it added to the pain they were enduring.

'Because of this, it's worse. It's more difficult to accept. If it had been a man, the first criminal act, you couldn't prevent it, but in this case they had been able to prevent it. That makes it double the pain,' says Hans-Peter.

'We have the luck that he's in prison now and we hope that he is never set free, but Manuela is still dead and nothing brings her back,' says Arlette. 'Manuela has no right and no possibility to come back and why should he have this right? It's not possible to forgive, ever. If it was her death because of an accident, we could forgive, but this is not to forgive,' says her father.

In Ireland, a person serving a life sentence will spend an average of 18 years in prison, but the Riedos do not believe that is enough for taking their daughter's life. They say they will be furious if they are ever informed that Barry is released from prison.

'It's not good. We would get angry; very angry. We cannot really imagine that Gerald Barry is set free some time. We just expect that the justice or the people recognise that this man is ill and he will do criminal acts again and again and again and it will never find an end. He will never change himself and the system should let him stay in prison until he dies. We wouldn't accept if he is set free,' says Arlette.

'We will visit Ireland again and again, but if we know that he is set free some day, we wouldn't visit Ireland again, as we are sure that the next tragedy is coming,' says Hans-Peter.

Hans-Peter was particularly close to Manuela and this was evident in the immediate aftermath of Barry's trial, when his victim impact statement was read out to the court. In the speech, which was translated from German to English for the court, Hans-Peter told how Manuela was their sunshine. 'You really can't put into words what the death of our beloved daughter Manuela has taken from us. You have robbed Manuela of sixty to seventy years of her life and taken the future away from us, her parents. I will never lead my daughter as a bride to the altar and my wife will never knit baby clothes for a grandchild and we won't have anyone to look after us when we are old,' he said.

'When Manuela was born, on 5 November 1989, a new challenge began for us as her parents. We were able then to give this tiny, helpless, beautiful child everything that parents should give: love, friendship, honesty, warmth, security and much more. We were able to watch Manuela grow up from a little baby to a unique, wonderful person. With her special manner she was loved and respected by everyone. She was a good friend, a good student, she was our pride and joy; and we were so happy to have such a daughter. These wonderful memories are all that is left for us,' said her distraught father.

After the court case was over, Hans-Peter was asked by journalists how he felt about Barry. His response was to draw a comparison with the devil. He said Barry was the devil and that the streets were a safer place without him. He still believes those words are true.

He smiles tenderly as he sits in the kitchen of their home and remembers the close bond he enjoyed with his daughter. 'She was our life. Father and daughter had a very, very close relationship. Until she was starting her education at the office, after she finished school, we were together seven days a week. We were never separated during the week. She finished school and started with this next education at the office,' he recalls.

He explains that Manuela was in the last of a three-year professional course, which her parents say was similar to a secretarial course. It involved spending two days in school and three days in an office. During her office training, she worked in a support centre for people being released from prison. It involved helping them to find jobs and homes and supporting them to stay out of trouble. Manuela's work, principally, was secretarial, such as writing reports, and she enjoyed the experience, as her mother explains, 'She enjoyed it very much. During her education, she visited a prison to see how it is to live in a prison. Someone broke the door because he was very angry about the service. He wasn't content with the money ... Her boss didn't want to give her this education place because he felt that she was too young, but she was older than her age. She was very mature and so she got this place.' Ironically, she would meet her death at the hands of man who had previously served time in prison, in Ireland. 'They help such people to start a new life after prison and such a guy killed her,' says Arlette.

After she had completed this course, Manuela had planned to go to San Diego in the US for a year to take a language course. She then hoped to study hotel management in a college near Bern. Even at the young age of 17, she had her future well planned out and was very eager to ensure her dreams would become a reality. But it was not to be. 'She had the form for San Diego, but she didn't send it. It was still here,' says her mother, sadly.

While her education was important to her, Manuela also believed in forming good relationships with people and was never slow to reach out and help others. Her kind nature was at the centre of her making contact with a four-year-old girl, under the World Vision programme. 'It was very important for her to deal with other people and not to make an education only with computers and paper and letters. She wanted to be in contact with people in her profession and because of this, she chose this special kind of work. At the age of fifteen, she decided that she wanted to be a good mother for a child from World Vision and she had contact with a child from World Vision, from Costa Rica. She was like a godmother. Every month from her income she spent fifty francs [on the child]. That's a lot because at the beginning of such education you earn three or five hundred francs, not more,' explains Hans-Peter.

In the aftermath of Gerald Barry being dealt with in the courts, Hans-Peter and Arlette were quoted in the media as referring to Manuela as their angel. This was in recognition of her love of angels since she was a small child. She collected angels and there are several figurines of angels in her parents' apartment. 'It's a symbol of protecting. It was the idea that everybody has a protecting angel. When we went on holidays, we bought an angel, like a protecting angel, for this holiday. Other school colleagues told Manuela, "You are our angel. We are so happy that you are with us because you are our angel",' says Arlette. Hans-Peter and Arlette firmly believe that Manuela was in the wrong place at the wrong time and was unlucky to have met her killer. They don't believe she felt any fear when she took the route where she was killed. 'I am sure that she wouldn't have taken this dark way at midnight, for example, but it was early in the evening and she wasn't a frightened person. It was seven o'clock,' says her father.

Her mother concurs with his view. 'She wasn't afraid normally. Take for example this street where she came from. The next little village is dark in the evening and she would go there alone and she wasn't afraid,' says Arlette.

———

In the wake of Manuela's death, fundraising concerts were organised in Galway and in her native Switzerland, in her memory. Among those who participated in the Galway concert were high-profile musicians and singers such as Sharon Shannon, Marc Roberts, Lucia Evans and Frank Naughton. Every morning, Arlette's day begins by walking into Manuela's bedroom and turning on songs from that selection of music. The music fills the apartment throughout the day and Arlette does not turn it off until the evening. It is her way of getting through the day and is her tribute to Manuela, while Hans-Peter is at work in Bern.

In February 2010, Hans-Peter and Arlette wrote a letter of appreciation to the people of Galway, thanking them for their support in the aftermath of their daughter's death and for their backing for the concert. In that letter, they expressed their wish that the €50,000 raised through the concert would be spent in Galway and the west of Ireland on causes that were close to Manuela's heart. The letter was sent to the organising committee of the Galway concert. They also sent photographs of Manuela's gravestone which carries the Claddagh symbol, emphasising the bond they feel has been created between them and the people of Galway.

'We would like to thank all those people who invested so much time preparing, presenting and performing the Night for Manuela concert. We would also like to thank the people from in and around Galway who attended the concert — without all your help this concert would not be as successful as it was. The organising committee of the Night for Manuela has informed us that over €50,000 was raised. It is now our wish that this money will remain and will be spent in Galway and the west of Ireland, supporting professional services and projects that do invaluable work, work that is at the heart of Manuela's Foundation. We look forward every day to returning to Galway — to our new friends and to Manuela,' they wrote. They signed the letter 'Arlette & Hans-Peter Riedo' and 'Our angel in Heaven, Manuela, rest in peace'. Hans-Peter and Arlette visited Galway in April 2010 when they told the people of the city that victims of sexual assault would benefit for years to come from the Foundation.

As they look to the future, Hans-Peter and Arlette are determined to stay strong, in their only daughter's memory. They visit her grave in the cemetery in Wohlen — a short distance from their home — every day, where they light candles and say prayers. When they cannot attend, such as when they are visiting Galway, they ensure that friends will visit Manuela's graveside and light candles.

'It's past and I move on to the future. The question remains, why did this happen, with Manuela? I'm her mother and I cannot let her go until now. I have open eyes and I always see things which remind me of Manuela. I cannot let her go,' says Arlette.

Susanne Nielen Gangwisch, who remains with the Riedos while they talk about Manuela, explains that Hans-Peter is recovering from the pain at a quicker pace than Arlette. 'She needs more time. He is one step ahead of Arlette,' she explains.

Asked how her brutal death has changed their lives, their answers are short, but say so much. 'We are no family any more,' says Hans-Peter. Arlette slowly adds, 'It's over.'

Chapter 2
The Good Samaritan

Finbar Dennehy had a heart of gold and that ultimately cost him his life. That is the view of his family, who believe that he was forced to pay the price for being a good Samaritan and kindly offering an acquaintance a place to stay for a few days.

A murder enquiry was launched by gardaí after the body of 50-year-old Mr Dennehy was discovered in his apartment in Clontarf, on the afternoon of Wednesday 26 September 2007. Mr Dennehy, a retired executive with Cadbury's, was single and lived alone in an apartment in a complex on Seafield Road in Clontarf. The alarm was raised after a friend became concerned when he was unable to contact him. Finbar's friend went to his apartment and found his body on a couch in the sitting room area. According to gardaí, there was no sign of a break-in to the apartment. A post-mortem examination showed that Finbar had suffered a violent death and had sustained a single stab wound. His hands had been tied and there was a bag over his head. Finbar had last been seen alive the previous Saturday night.

As gardaí investigated the death of Mr Dennehy, they took various statements from those known to him. A major

breakthrough in their investigation came three days after the
discovery of his body, when a 41-year-old man, Michael
Downes, was arrested at a guesthouse in Dublin city on
Saturday evening, 29 September. He was held for questioning,
before being charged in connection with the death, on Monday
1 October. Downes, then of no fixed abode, was brought before
Dublin District Court, charged with assault causing serious
harm to Mr Dennehy. (In cases such as this, the State will often
bring a lesser charge, and a more serious charge is brought after
sufficient evidence has been gathered.) The court was told that
Downes had not lived at his original home in Ennis, Co. Clare
for a considerable period of time. Downes was remanded in
custody to appear again in court a week later.

At a later stage, Downes was charged with murdering Mr
Dennehy and was returned for trial to the Central Criminal
Court. In October 2008, Downes (then aged 42) pleaded guilty
to murdering Mr Dennehy, between 24 and 26 September 2007,
and was sentenced to life in jail.

Finbar's brother, Tony, who agreed to talk to me for this
book, tells me that Finbar's final years were his happiest, having
told those close to him that he was gay. While Tony knew, for
many years, that Finbar was gay, he had not come out until
three years before his tragic death. 'He came out. He was senior
management in Cadbury's. He retired and he got into the gay
scene. He was a very innocent man. He was truly happy. For the
first time in his life, he was really, really happy. Close friends
would say when he came out, he really blossomed. That was
three years before he died. He met lovely people, lovely friends.
He might have come out, but he didn't wear his gayness on his
sleeve like a badge. Very few people knew he was gay. Close
family and cousins didn't know. It was a shock to them that he
was gay,' says Tony.

Finbar was an independent man and while he kept in regular
contact with his family, months would often pass without them
seeing him. Telephone calls were a regular part of his weekly

routine, however. Tony, who lived just 20 minutes away from Finbar, would regularly ring him and on hearing his voice, would be reassured that he was well. Tony recalls speaking to Finbar just hours before his death, but says there was no indication that anything was wrong.

'We saw very little of him. We didn't live in each other's ears. I used to ring him every couple of weeks to make sure he was OK. I rang him that Monday, the 24th [September, 2007]. He was sleepy. He was tired. Once I heard his voice, I felt he was OK. Little did I realise he had company at that time. I'm assuming Downes was there. He said he was OK. I said I'd ring him later.' The phone records show it was a very short conversation. He was an intensely private man. You wouldn't call down to him, uninvited,' Tony says.

Finbar Dennehy trusted Michael Downes enough to offer him a place to stay for a few days. Little did he know that, just hours after he made his generous offer, Downes would murder him. Finbar Dennehy could also not have known that this acquaintance had a long history of violence, although even those who knew him from a young age could not believe that he was capable of taking a life.

———

By the time Michael Downes murdered Finbar Dennehy in September 2007, he had accumulated a string of convictions, many involving violence or the threat of violence. The most serious of these were the robbery of an elderly woman in Ennis, Co. Clare and the attempted robbery of a woman in Gort, Co. Galway; both in 2003.

Downes, who came from Marian Avenue in Ennis, was known to gardaí in his native county for several years, during which time he amassed a number of convictions. At 4 a.m. on the night of 27 January 2003, he broke into the home of his

82-year-old neighbour. He tied her up and threatened to kill her. Downes wore a handkerchief across his face and socks on his hands when he broke into the woman's home. She woke up to see Downes standing over her, with a knife in his hand.

A garda told the court hearing in relation to that case that Downes threatened his victim with the knife and demanded to know where her money was. She showed him her purse, which contained €40 from her old age pension. Downes tied her up with shoe laces and searched for more money. Before he left her house with €40, he untied her and warned her that he would kill her if she told anyone what had happened.

The incident terrified the woman, who had regarded Downes as a neighbour and a friend. But, as he would do to Finbar Dennehy a few years later, Downes betrayed this woman's trust and friendship. At Ennis Circuit Court in October of that year, he pleaded guilty to the robbery of the woman and was jailed for three years. The judge in the case said he would impose a three-year jail term because a guilty plea had been entered by Downes.

On 25 April 2003, just three months after the robbery of his neighbour, Downes walked into Gillane's bakery, The Square, Gort, with a knife in his hand. A 59-year-old woman was alone in the shop, as it was late in the afternoon. He was dressed in black clothing and wore sunglasses. He pointed the knife at the woman and told her to open the cash register, but she pretended not to hear him. He repeated his order, but the woman walked away from the counter and pretended to call the gardaí on her mobile phone.

The case was heard before Galway Circuit Court in November 2003 — just weeks after Downes had been jailed for three years at Ennis Circuit Court — and was told that Downes panicked when he believed the woman was calling the gardaí. He ran from the shop and the shopkeeper pursued him down the street. He was seen running into a hostel, where he was arrested by gardaí a short time later. According to gardaí, he was not aggressive and he admitted the offence. The court was told that while the woman stood up to Downes, she had feared for her life and was nervous after the incident. However, she had since made a recovery.

Downes' barrister said his client had had issues with drugs and alcohol and had a history of psychiatric illness. He put it to the judge that the attempted robbery had been an act of stupidity and that Downes had been out of his head with tablets at the time. He had needed money to feed his habit and had resorted to robbery, said the barrister.

The judge praised the shopkeeper for the great presence of mind and degree of coolness she had displayed when confronted by a man with a knife. He said she was entitled to enjoy the freedom to run her business without having to face attack. He said it was a very serious offence and imposed a three-year prison sentence. However, two of the three years were suspended, because Downes had pleaded guilty, while the remaining sentence was backdated to April 2003, when Downes had gone into custody for the robbery of the woman in Ennis.

Downes served his sentence and was released from prison in March 2006. However, it wasn't long before he crept onto the garda radar again, falsely imprisoning a man and stealing a credit card and money at an apartment in Ennis on 6 May 2006. That offence occurred just two months after his release from prison. Downes went to the home of the man, with whom he was acquainted, pulled him by the throat and ordered him to turn off his mobile phone. A violent struggle ensued. Downes got a knife from the kitchen and ordered the man to hand over his credit card and PIN number. When the man refused to do so, Downes attacked him. The victim handed over his credit card and €45 and screamed for help. Downes bound the man's hands and feet with cable and apron strings. He put a shirt on the man's head and stuffed pieces of material into his mouth, in an effort to prevent him from shouting for help.

He told his terrified victim that if the PIN number he had

given him was incorrect, he had a knife and he would return and cut him. Fortunately for the victim, neighbours heard his cries and contacted gardaí, who quickly arrived on the scene. A garda told the court hearing in October 2008 that he banged on the door of the apartment on arrival there, but it wasn't opened for six or seven minutes. The occupant of the flat eventually opened the door, having been untied.

When the case came to court, Downes' barrister submitted that he had issues with alcohol and prescription-drug abuse and an apology was made in court to the victim. Downes, who had worked in the bar trade in the past, was unemployed at the time. The judge heard that Downes had 11 previous convictions — which were described as mostly public-order matters — and said he was satisfied the defendant had a propensity for violence. A lengthy sentence was appropriate, to protect the public from Downes, said the judge.

Downes was handed a six-year jail term for each charge, false imprisonment and theft, to run concurrently for what a judge called a 'terrifying' ordeal for the victim. The final two years were suspended, on condition that Downes enter a bond to keep the peace.

Downes was not charged in relation to this incident until Friday 5 October 2007 — over a week after the murder of Mr Dennehy. He was brought before a sitting of Ennis District Court, which was told that a bench warrant had been issued for Downes at Kilrush District Court in January 2007. The bench warrant had been issued after Downes failed to appear in court to face a charge of assaulting a man in Kilrush, in October 2006. The bench warrant was executed on 5 October 2007. However, the assault charge was later withdrawn.

Just weeks before he murdered Mr Dennehy, Michael Downes committed another serious offence in Dublin. Towards the end of August 2007, he met a man outside a pub in Dalkey, where they were both smoking. Downes told the man he had nowhere to stay and asked if he could stay with him. The man agreed and they got a taxi back to his house. The victim then gave Downes his bank card and PIN number, along with his house keys, to go to the off-licence for alcohol. However, Downes did not return to the man's house. Instead, during the following week, he withdrew €832 from the man's bank account. A few days later, the man reported the incident to his bank and he then learned that Downes had taken money out of his account. Downes was seen on CCTV footage using the bank card. He later pleaded guilty to the theft of the man's money and was given a two-year jail sentence.

Downes' activities became more violent. On 10 August 2007, he falsely imprisoned and robbed a man in Grangegorman, Dublin. The victim came in contact with Downes after replying to a message he had left on a gay chatline. The victim would later tell gardaí he invited Downes to his apartment, having met him briefly some days earlier. While in the apartment, Downes told the victim to get undressed. The man complied with the request, before Downes produced a kitchen knife and forced the man to lie face down on the couch, telling him, 'Don't fight me, if you fight me I'll f**king kill you.' Downes then tied the man up and stole his wallet and ATM card. He demanded the PIN number for the ATM card and said he would cut the man to bits and would 'cut his nuts off' if the PIN number was incorrect. Downes left the apartment and the victim managed to unravel the ties, before raising the alarm.

Downes' barrister told the court that his client came from a small town, where his sexual orientation was not common, and that he was troubled by this. A ten-year sentence was handed down by a judge, who said that Downes' personal difficulties could not explain why he had committed the offence.

––––

Downes' violence moved to a new level in September 2007, when an attack, tragically, had fatal consequences. Giving evidence to the court, a garda involved in the investigation said that Downes and Finbar Dennehy knew each other. He said that Downes had travelled to Dublin on the Sunday before the murder and had arranged to meet Finbar. They had socialised in various public houses, before returning to Finbar's apartment that evening. Details of the circumstances of Finbar's death were revealed to the court, which was told that he had been 'tied up elaborately on the couch, a plastic bag was tied over his head and there was a pool of blood on the floor beside him.' Finbar had died from strangulation and a stab wound to the groin.

Downes told gardaí he had been with Finbar in his apartment the previous Monday and 'a dispute had arisen in relation to sex.' He said he had got a knife from the kitchen, went to the living room area and asked Finbar for money. A struggle ensued and according to Downes, he tied up Finbar on the couch. He claimed that he had stayed in the apartment that night and strangled him the following morning, with what Finbar's family believe was the cord from his dressing gown. Finbar's family believe he had allowed Downes to sleep in his bedroom in the one-bed apartment, while he slept on the couch.

In a victim impact statement which was read to the Central Criminal Court, Finbar's sister Phyllis described him as a gentle person, who had died terrified and alone. She said her brother had never wanted to be front-page news.

Tony Dennehy fights back the tears as he recalls the lonely death his brother suffered and says he cannot forgive Michael Downes. Tony feels that a failure in the system paved the way for Michael Downes to kill his brother and says that if stiffer sentences had been handed down for the other offences he committed, Downes would not have had the opportunity to kill Finbar. Tony Dennehy recalls the events which led up to the grim discovery of his brother's body. 'Wednesday came and friends of Finbar were worried about him. He had actually confided in one of them that he had met this man in The George [public house] four or five weeks previously. He said his name was Mick. He was from the country. He had lost his job. He had nowhere to stay; a typical hard luck story. He [Finbar] said this to a friend of his and his friend said, "Be very careful. You don't know his second name. You don't know where he's from. You don't know why he lost his job. You don't know why he lost his digs. If he's looking for somewhere to stay, send him to a hostel." Finbar got quite defensive, because he could be quite strong-willed. He was very kind. I think he came out and he found the world was a wonderful place. Who could have known that Michael Downes would do what he did?'

Tony does not believe that the two men were romantically linked, even though Downes told gardaí that a dispute had arisen over sex. He believes it was a case of Finbar showing his kind, decent side and offering Downes a place to stay. He also believes that Downes had never stayed with Finbar prior to this one visit.

'No. Oh, no. I don't think Finbar ever had a partner in his whole life. They met about a month or six weeks earlier in The George and they exchanged phone numbers. The papers made it out like it was a romantic liaison. It wasn't,' he says.

Over the past few years, Tony Dennehy has invested much energy in attempting to find answers to questions that haunt him, relating to his brother's death. While he firmly believes that Finbar was forced to pay the ultimate price for simply offering kindness and generosity to Michael Downes, he is curious about the circumstances surrounding the fateful meeting of the two men. How had Finbar been so unlucky to have met Downes? Tony believes that Downes texted his brother early on Sunday 23 September 2007, and told him that he was in Belfast. He believes Downes told Finbar that he was due to arrive in Dublin later that day and the two arranged to meet. Tony believes that the two men met that Sunday at Busáras in Dublin and spent the afternoon in a number of pubs, before going back to Finbar's apartment.

'It wouldn't be unusual for people to stay in Finbar's

apartment. It was a one-bed apartment. Finbar would sleep on the couch. We know that Michael Downes stayed there on the Sunday night. We are fairly sure of that. On Monday, I rang him at about twenty to one. I heard his voice and I thought he was OK. He cancelled an appointment on Monday. He cancelled another appointment on Wednesday, saying that his friend was staying over another night, Monday night. Tuesday came and went. On Wednesday, one of his friends got very concerned. He went down to the apartment. He actually had a key to the front door because Finbar had got a new bathroom in [some time previously]. He was away on holidays and he gave this guy the key to let the builder in.

'His friend went down and opened the front door. Immediately he knew there was something wrong. The light was on in the bathroom. You know when you put a light on in a bathroom, the fan comes on. That used to drive Finbar insane,' Tony recalls.

Tony speaks at length about his brother, but whilst the happy memories are accompanied by laughter, Finbar's violent death brings back so many sad thoughts. As he battles with tears, Tony clearly remembers the scene at his brother's home in the aftermath of his death. 'His friend could see a portable house phone lying on a phone book in the bathroom, by the toilet seat. Finbar's suitcase was askew. It wasn't at the wall. He went down to the dining room/sitting room and he couldn't get in. The door into the lounge was locked. He immediately sensed there was something wrong, because that door is never locked. He vaguely could make out something on the couch. He called the guards and the guards came. They couldn't get the door open, so they called the fire brigade. The fire brigade came and they broke down the door and immediately the guards put everybody out and said it was a crime scene.

'Michael Downes left a perfect crime scene. He locked the door. Once the door was open, the only ones there were the guards and the firemen. On Wednesday night it was on the news that a man had been found dead in an apartment block in Clontarf. We were totally oblivious. Thursday morning came and I was talking to my sister in England. She put the phone down. I put the phone down. The phone rang again. I left it ring out. I'd be a bit like that. Then it rang again and I answered it. She was absolutely hysterical. She said that friends in Cadbury's were after ringing her to say that something had happened to Finbar.'

Although the Dennehys were not told immediately that Finbar had been killed, Tony had that sixth sense. He just knew that something was wrong. He will never forget the panic and hysteria that set in around this time. 'So I rang a very close friend of Finbar's. I knew by the way he answered the phone, he said, "Tony, something has happened, but it's not my place to tell you." I didn't know whether I was being wound up or what. I rang the guards in Clontarf and the guard asked me to identify myself. I knew there was something up straight away. He put me on to a senior detective. He asked me to identify myself and I did. He said, "I'm very, very sorry. I can't say anything more to you on the phone. I have a victim liaison officer and a guard on their way out to you. I know it's difficult, but please wait." I knew he was dead. I just did. I could sense it. I could feel it. The guards arrived out at my house. They told me that they had found a body in my brother's apartment and that there was a plastic bag on the head. They couldn't be certain that it was Finbar, but they strongly suspected that it was. The only one who could positively prove that it was Finbar was me.'

That was Thursday afternoon, 27 September, and while it was suspected that the body was that of his brother, no formal identification had taken place. However, that afternoon, Finbar was named by other media sources. This added to the family's trauma. They had yet to identify Finbar and had not seen his body; yet his name was in the public domain. To say that this deeply upset the Dennehy family is an understatement.

As Tony explains, 'On Thursday night, there were people

pouring in and out. They actually wanted me to do the identification that night, but it was an extremely complicated post-mortem. They wouldn't be ready for me to identify Finbar until the following morning at nine o'clock.

'I was up all night,' he tells me, frustration etched across his face. 'We got down to the morgue. I wanted to get in to identify him. I was actually losing my nerve about identifying him. So I went in. The morgue technician offered his condolences. Suddenly the door is open and there he is, lying on a trolley, with a white sheet around him. I knew it was him straight away.'

Tony says, 'It was a bit of a blur after that. It's something I don't ever wish on anybody to have to do; to see your own flesh and blood like that. They told me he died from a stab wound to the femoral artery, the groin. Once the femoral artery is slashed, you lose a massive amount of blood. You lose consciousness within four or five seconds and you bleed to death, rapidly.'

Tony is particularly upset about the conditions in which Finbar's post-mortem was carried out. 'The morgue was actually a Portakabin, like you would find on a building site. It's a temporary structure. It was the most disgraceful, disgusting building I was ever in in my life. For a man who wore Gucci clothes and was spotlessly clean and everything about him, paid his taxes all his life, never upset anybody. This man had stolen his life and the State was after taking whatever dignity was left. I desperately wanted him home, because no-one loved him that weekend. I couldn't grieve for my brother. I tried to keep it together to look after my sisters.'

———

Once the details of the post-mortem examination became known, gardaí then launched a murder investigation. Given that there was no sign of a forced entry to Finbar's home, this prompted his family and friends to conclude that he was killed by someone he knew. One name quickly sprang to the minds of those close to him: Michael Downes.

Although Finbar's friends had not met Downes, they strongly suspected that he was involved in his death. 'Friends of Finbar said they wanted to come out to the house that night and talk to me and they did. It was then that it emerged that he had met this guy, Mick. I remember saying to one of his friends that night, "Do you think this guy Mick killed him?" He said, "I've no doubt in the world this guy killed him,"' says Tony.

'The body was released the following Friday. Apparently, they needed the body to get as much forensic evidence as they could. Much as I wanted him home, what could they do? Anything that would help convict; I wasn't going to stand in the guards' way. That Friday, the undertaker took me aside and said, "It's been eleven days. We don't know if you can have an open coffin." Once you do a post-mortem, decay sets in rapidly. Eleven days is a long time,' he says, clearly haunted by the painful memory.

'He was buried the following Monday, so I decided there would be no removal. I was afraid of the press. He was brought straight from the undertakers to the church in Clontarf. That two weeks was just the most awful two weeks of my life. Finbar had been alive all night, tied up, gagged. A gangland killing is over in three seconds. My brother was alive all night at the hands of a monster,' Tony says.

Once Finbar's funeral was over and his cremation had taken place, his heartbroken family and friends could then focus on ensuring that justice was done. Just one year later, on 7 October 2008, Downes was jailed for life, after he admitted murdering Finbar. As Tony explains, 'We were blessed that there was no trial. We knew that he was going to plead guilty. The guards said to me about three or four weeks before, that there was every indication that he was going to plead guilty.' Tony knew that Downes could have changed his mind right up to the last minute, but when he appeared, he pleaded guilty. Nonetheless, the court appearance was distressing for the Dennehy family, as Tony explains. 'What upset us hugely was the fact that the prosecuting counsel asked the garda sergeant to go into the witness box to give Michael Downes' account of events that night, where he said there was a dispute over sex . . . That murderer wrote my brother's epitaph in court. I could have torn my hair out,' Tony says. Although Downes pleaded guilty to murder, Tony still feels that he never showed any remorse for the killing. 'No. He's a monster. He was in court that day and didn't show any remorse, any expression of grief. Nothing. He didn't need to kill him. He could have walked out that door the following morning and that would have been the end of it. All I can do is thank the guards who got the man who did it.'

———

Tony Dennehy doesn't entirely believe Downes' account of what happened on the day he killed Finbar and that has motivated him to find out more information. However, he has faced many barriers and is deeply upset that he could not see the Book of Evidence.

'We have never got the Book of Evidence. Nothing. Victims should be allowed to see the Book of Evidence, but they are not. You reach a point where you have to let certain things go or you will drive yourself mad. I feel just totally failed by here [this country]. I own a little place in France. People say to me, well the same thing could happen in France, but it hasn't,' he says.

Tony Dennehy does not believe Downes' assertion that a dispute arose over sex and refers to a letter his solicitor received from the deputy state pathologist, Dr Michael Curtis, confirming that there was nothing found at the scene to indicate a sexual motive. In the letter, dated 4 June 2009, Dr Curtis stated, 'My opinion relating to the specific points raised therein is as follows: 1. There were no specific findings either on examination of the scene of death or at the subsequent post-mortem examination to indicate a sexual motive behind the murder of Mr Dennehy. 2. I do not believe that Mr Dennehy contributed in any way to his own death. 3. There were no specific features to indicate sexual depravity or perversion.'

Tony Dennehy says his family is deeply upset that Downes' account of Finbar's death was not disputed in court. 'If it had gone to trial, the deputy state pathologist would have been requested to give evidence. It causes us enormous anguish, as a family, that Michael Downes' version of events came out in court and was allowed to go unchallenged. The deputy state pathologist clearly stated there was no evidence from the scene and no evidence from the subsequent post-mortem of any sexual activity whatsoever. Michael Downes said that they had gone back to my brother's apartment on Monday evening and that there was a dispute about sex. He took a knife from the drawer. He then tied my brother up, kept him alive all night and left the following morning. Before he left the following morning, he strangled him. He says Finbar was alive all night,' says Tony.

For the Dennehy family, nothing hurts more than knowing that Michael Downes was walking the streets, despite the serious crimes he had committed prior to killing Finbar. Tony believes that the sentences imposed on Downes for his previous violent crimes were not adequate and feels if they had been tougher, his brother would still be alive.

'I am very, very angry. I am very angry about the case in Gort. If he had served that sentence on top of the sentence he was serving for attacking the elderly woman in Ennis, my brother would be alive today. He has now racked up other sentences. All that does is insult me. It dilutes my brother's sentence. It dilutes the punishment that Michael Downes should have received. It has destroyed us as a family. For what? I think it's a failure of the system, but I don't see it changing in my lifetime,' he says.

What angers Tony Dennehy most about the murder of his brother? 'The fact that he [Downes] was out there, on bail. And the lenient sentences. If someone came to me and said, "I tied an elderly woman up. I broke into her house and I robbed her," what would you expect to get? I'd say if you don't get fifteen years to life you would be lucky. He got three years. I blame the judiciary. I think they have gone soft on crime,' he says.

'I just think that sentences should be more severe. Concurrent sentences should be wiped out. Concurrent sentencing is an insult and means nothing. Suspended sentencing means nothing. I think there should be more mandatory sentencing, with more mandatory minimum sentences for serious crime. In the kindest possible way, I do believe that hearing these cases, one after another, every day, it is easily possible for a judge to become desensitised. The human misery and destroyed lives left in their wake is enormous. A court would have to see that to take it into account. Life should mean that, and if it does not, do not call it that,' says Tony.

Tony is adamant that, 'I will do everything I can to keep him [Downes] in jail for as long as I can. I don't think he should ever get out again. I have to be notified if he goes before the Parole Board,' Tony says.

And even though the name Michael Downes will be forever etched in their minds, for all the wrong reasons; for all the horrific memories of Finbar's death, his family is very keen to focus on the kind, gentle man that he was. The fond memories will help those close to him to get on with their lives. Finbar, who turned 50 on 13 September 2007 — just days before he was murdered — was a man who thrived on perfection.

'Finbar was extremely private. He was a very shy, gentle nervous man. If someone hit me, I would hit back. Finbar, I know, would run a mile from a fight. I know he said to Michael Downes that night, "Take anything, just don't rob me. Don't hurt me". I know that was the way Finbar would have handled it. He was such a gentle man. I loved him. He was a very orderly man. Everything was perfect. That was the way he was,' says Tony.

When Tony talks about his brother, it's clear how much he admired him: 'He was very much into table tennis. He was very good at it. He loved bowling. He loved a gin and tonic and a laugh. He was a great talker, a real raconteur. He worked hard. He had worked with Cadbury's for thirty years. He started there as a post boy and worked his way up to financial director. He went back to DCU [Dublin City University] and took a degree in Business Studies. He was a taxpayer, who never harmed anybody in his life. He was flying to South Africa the following Friday to visit friends,' Tony tells me.

'He was a very charming man; very funny and very witty. I'd ring him on a Monday night at half-seven. He could tell you were ringing him to check up on him. He wouldn't like that. He would say, "Are you ringing me about anything special because I'm missing *Fair City* now! I'll talk to you later," and he would be gone.

'But he had a heart of gold. Tragically that cost him his life. He thought he was doing Michael Downes a favour,' says Tony.

'It has broken my heart. They are just words. But it has. I look out there and nothing is the same any more. For a long time I couldn't feel good about anything. I felt guilty. I felt, how could you enjoy something when Finbar's dead? I try and do things that are positive. I go to France. I lie in the sun. I do a bit of gardening. But I'll never forget it. The problem is the nightmares. My brother is at peace now. Whatever he suffered, nobody can hurt him now.'

Chapter 3
A Fateful Encounter

It was a birthday celebration that ended in tragedy. To mark her 33rd birthday, Sylvia Roche-Kelly joined friends for a night out in her native city, Limerick, on Friday 7 December 2007. Having grown up in Limerick, the mother-of-two was familiar with the city and treated herself to a rare night out.

Sylvia, who grew up in Coonagh, Limerick, ran her own art gallery in Sixmilebridge, where she lived and cared for her two young children, a son aged twelve and a four-year-old girl. She had lived at Ballintlea, between Cratloe and Sixmilebridge, and had recently separated from her husband, Lorcan Roche-Kelly.

While socialising with her sister and friends, Sylvia bumped into a young man in Ted's nightclub. It appeared, on the face of it, no more than an innocent encounter, but just hours later he would murder her in a hotel bedroom.

———

Staff at the Clarion Hotel on Steamboat Quay in Limerick City were horrified to discover a body in one of their hotel rooms, at around midday on Saturday 8 December 2007. Staff found a naked body, lying face down in a bath in one of the hotel's rooms. Clothing belonging to a woman was found in the hotel bedroom. The woman was identified as Sylvia Roche-Kelly.

However, the man who had booked into the room the previous evening was nowhere to be seen. The man was later identified as Jerry McGrath, a 23-year-old from Tipperary. He had disappeared, without checking out of the hotel.

Gardaí were swiftly notified and an investigation was immediately launched, while a post-mortem examination was carried out. Although the initial results of tests carried out on the body proved inconclusive, gardaí revealed that Sylvia had died as a result of an assault.

Gardaí at Henry Street in Limerick city had a very serious investigation on their hands. They were tasked with piecing together Sylvia's movements in the hours prior to her death. They were also keen to establish the whereabouts of McGrath and to investigate the link between Sylvia and her killer. How had they come into contact with each other? As the investigation progressed, gardaí obtained CCTV footage, which showed McGrath leaving the Clarion Hotel on the morning Sylvia's body was discovered. Other CCTV footage from the city showed the two walking hand-in-hand through the streets of Limerick in the early hours of the morning, before arriving at the Clarion Hotel at around 3 a.m.

I spoke to a senior officer involved in the investigation, who explains, 'It was a Saturday the body was found. The hotel had a fantastic CCTV system and immediately we were able to trace her from that CCTV system, going into the room with an individual, so the investigation, from that minute on, and at a really early stage, focused on identifying him and then tracing him.' Further tests were carried out on the body and a murder investigation was launched by gardaí.

Gardaí concluded that McGrath had fled the jurisdiction. As the garda explains, 'He skipped it to England fairly immediately and we made contact with him through relations of his. His family was very co-operative with us. They would have been disgusted and shocked at what he did and they persuaded him to come home, back to Ireland. Early on in the investigation, as a result of trawling through CCTV footage from the city centre, we established that she had left Ted's nightclub with him. We knew she hadn't gone there with him, from interviewing her friends, so we knew it was just a chance meeting and they went back to the hotel he was staying in,' says the senior garda.

On Tuesday evening, 11 December, after he returned to Ireland, McGrath was arrested. He was taken to Henry Street garda station, where he was detained for questioning. On Wednesday 12 December, McGrath was charged with murdering Sylvia Roche-Kelly at the Clarion Hotel, on Saturday 8 December, and was brought before Limerick District Court on Thursday morning, 13 December. McGrath, of Ballywalter, Cashel, Co. Tipperary, was remanded in custody, to re-appear in court the following Tuesday and was later returned for trial to the Central Criminal Court.

Meanwhile, as the communities of Sixmilebridge, Cratloe and Coonagh were slowly coming to terms with what had happened, Sylvia was fondly remembered at her funeral that week. Hundreds of mourners, both from her native Limerick and her adopted Sixmilebridge, turned out to pay their respects at her funeral Mass at the Little Church, Sixmilebridge, on the Wednesday morning following her death. Cratloe parish priest, Fr Liam Enright, told mourners how Sylvia's tragic death had shocked and saddened everyone.

'It doesn't make sense. It doesn't seem fair. Her great work is cut short. We are left with a terrible sense of loss. We are plunged into darkness. Tragic death, which is almost always sudden, is like a blackout. One minute the sun is shining. Next minute it is dark night. Without the slightest warning, or the slightest chance to prepare ourselves, we are plunged into an impenetrable darkness. In the space of a minute, our whole world is turned upside down. Nothing can prepare us for something like this, or save us from its devastating effects,' he said.

'Naturally we ask, why did it happen? There is a tendency to say, "It's the will of God". Let us be perfectly clear: God did not want this tragedy to happen. There is only one thing we can do. Just as when a blackout occurs, we rush for a light, any light, even that of a humble candle, so now we rush to the only light that can penetrate this awful darkness, namely, the light of Christ,' said Fr Enright.

Sylvia's tragic death had shocked not only her family and friends, but also the wider community. Sylvia was well known in the Sixmilebridge and Cratloe localities and had immersed herself in the local community. Friends recall how she had a tremendous enthusiasm and energy and readily involved herself in community activities. She ran an art gallery in Sixmilebridge until shortly before her death. She had closed the premises, but had continued to focus on her love of art through presenting art classes. It was her dream to re-open a gallery at a later stage and those who knew her and admired her determination believed she would achieve this.

'She went out to celebrate her 33rd birthday last Friday night and was looking forward to going for her night out, as she had not been in a while ...' Father Enright said at the funeral. 'Christ, too, died at the young age of 33,' he said. 'We must not dwell too much on the manner of her death. It is better to give thanks to God for her life and commend her to God in death.' Sylvia's husband Lorcan Roche-Kelly read out a poem in her memory, at the end of her funeral Mass, some of the words of which were, 'For I have loved you'; a tribute to the woman he loved.

———

The garda investigation into Sylvia's death took several months, as every piece of evidence was gathered. In March 2008, McGrath was sent forward for trial to the Central Criminal Court in Dublin. The case was listed for trial on 12 January 2009; some 13 months after Sylvia's death. McGrath pleaded guilty and the mandatory life sentence was handed down.

During the investigation, McGrath told gardaí that he had had sex with Sylvia in the hotel bedroom. McGrath told gardaí that he killed Sylvia after comments made during a conversation between the two angered him. There were just two people in the room that fateful morning. The only explanation available came from McGrath and gardaí had to include this in the case file. However, there is no way of proving that this is exactly what happened and gardaí believe there was more to it.

A senior garda involved in the investigation talked to me about McGrath's explanation for his assault on Sylvia Roche-Kelly. 'A certain version of it came out, that he gave us, that he had allegedly made these comments to her, but no-one can ever say whether that was the truth or not. People do say this kind of stuff to us and we have to record it and it is given then [in evidence], but it's only one side of the story. We couldn't ever be sure. To this day, I wouldn't believe that he told her about his involvement with the child down in Dundrum [it would later be revealed that, just months before killing Sylvia Roche-Kelly in Limerick, McGrath had falsely imprisoned a five-year-old girl in Dundrum, Co. Tipperary] and that she made a comment. But I might be wrong. How can you ever say yea or nay?' says the garda.

'There aren't too many people who are going to meet a person and, within an hour or two, tell them they had tried to take a child out of a house. Who is going to do that? That's just what he said, but that doesn't mean it's true. You might tell a friend of yours, through drink or whatever, that you did this thing, that it was building up, but I can't imagine any person doing that. Did he just flip on the night, having taken her back to the room? Nobody will ever know, really. There were only two of them and there wasn't CCTV in the room.

'It was a pure chance meeting on the night. She was out socialising. She was with her sister and friends. She was totally unlucky. She could have been any one of thousands of people who were out in Limerick that night and to meet the one person who was going to kill her. She came from a nightclub where there is never any trouble. A respectable crowd goes in there. To think, this chance meeting, how awful it was,' says the garda.

McGrath admitted hitting Sylvia Roche-Kelly in the face, pulling her hair, putting his hands around her neck and throttling her in the bed. He told gardaí that he may have kicked her between the legs with some force, before moving her body to the bath.

A garda told the Central Criminal Court that blood-stained towels were found at Sylvia's head and shoulders, while blood was also found on the bed and on the carpet beside the bed.

A post-mortem examination concluded that death was due to manual asphyxiation. Sylvia had sustained extensive bruising to the upper body, head and face, while she had also suffered a broken nose. The court was told she had sustained a vigorous and serious assault. Gardaí found DNA evidence confirming a sexual encounter.

The court was told that McGrath had one previous conviction, for assault causing harm to a female taxi driver in Cavan in April 2007. He was on bail for that offence when he killed Sylvia and was sentenced to nine months in jail for it in January 2008. And, just one month after he was jailed for life for Sylvia's murder, he was jailed for ten years for falsely imprisoning a five-year-old girl in Dundrum, Co. Tipperary, on 9 October 2007. This occurred just two months before he murdered Sylvia Roche-Kelly.

The profound impact Sylvia's death had on her family was in evidence through the victim impact statements that were read out to the court by a garda. In them, her parents, Esther and

John Bourke, described how they couldn't begin to explain the suffering and pain they had been forced to endure as a result of their daughter's death. They found it difficult to cope without her in their lives. Her mother wished to hold her in her arms again and tell her that she loved her, while her father said he spent most days thinking about her. They explained how they couldn't imagine that they would outlive their young daughter. Sylvia's husband, Lorcan Roche-Kelly, outlined how he had to explain to two young children that their mammy was dead and they would never see her again. He said they were devastated by Sylvia's death and explained how Sylvia's son — who was Lorcan's stepson — suffered from an autistic disorder and the only constant he had in his life was his mother.

An apology from McGrath was read out by his lawyer. He said he was truly sorry for what he had done and he would never forgive himself. At the end of the case, Sixmilebridge-based solicitor Gwen Bowen read a statement on behalf of Sylvia's family, outside the Four Courts. She described Sylvia as a 'warm, caring and wonderful mother', who was 'loving, enthusiastic and exuberant. This is how she will be remembered.' She said that Sylvia's family and community had suffered a profound loss and the impact on her children was immeasurable.

Sylvia's heartbroken family left Dublin that evening, knowing that her killer was facing a life sentence in prison.

———

A month later, McGrath pleaded guilty to the false imprisonment of the five-year-old in Dundrum, assault causing harm and burglary, relating to the incident. The ten-year sentence was handed down at Clonmel Circuit Court in February 2009, which heard that McGrath had gone into the bedroom of a five-year-old girl and squeezed her throat with his hands, before trying to carry her out of the house. The incident happened at 3.30 a.m., after McGrath had broken into the girl's parents' house.

The alarm was raised when the girl's mother woke up and saw McGrath with her daughter. She began to shout and McGrath tried to leave the house. However, the front door was locked and the girl's father managed to hold on to him until gardaí arrived.

McGrath's actions forced the little girl's parents to face a horrendous ordeal. Their shock and anger were outlined at the court hearing. Her father recalled, 'This is the worst crime a parent can imagine. To come so close to losing our daughter but succeeding in protecting her is both deeply frightening and joyful. The sight of McGrath running around the house with our daughter in his arms will remain with my wife for the rest of her life.' The court heard that the little girl's feeling of security in her own home and bedroom had been robbed from her and she regularly asked her parents, 'What was this mad man going to do with me?'

McGrath's lawyer said his client came from a respectable family. He said he had suffered from addiction to alcohol and had lost a child with a partner. McGrath's plea of guilty was taken into account and a ten-year jail sentence was handed down for false imprisonment. He was sentenced to eight years for burglary and four years for assault causing harm. All sentences would run concurrently.

At this stage, McGrath had been sentenced in respect of the murder in Limerick, the attack on the taxi driver in Cavan and the false imprisonment in Tipperary. These were all very serious crimes and took place within a relatively short period of time. The attack on the taxi driver was in April 2007. This was followed by the false imprisonment of the child six months later, in October, while the murder was two months after that, in December 2007.

It was while he was on bail, having been charged with the

assault of a female taxi driver in Cavan, that McGrath murdered
Sylvia. Once all the information on McGrath's criminal record
was in the public domain, it led to much reaction, not least
from Sylvia Roche-Kelly's husband, Lorcan. Following the court
case in Tipperary, he said the circumstances of the cases raised
'more profoundly serious questions over the decisions to grant
him bail.

'By twice granting bail to this extremely dangerous person,
the State gave him freedom, which he used as an opportunity
to murder Sylvia. The impact of her murder on those who
had already suffered so greatly at the hands of Jerry McGrath
must have been horrific,' he said, in a statement released to
the media.

Mr Roche-Kelly spoke on RTÉ radio the following week,
during which he asked why McGrath was let free, having
committed serious crimes, before he murdered Sylvia. There
were many questions, he said, and he was looking for answers.
'Why was he allowed bail?' he asked. He said he was keen to get
explanations because his daughter would one day want to know
what had happened.

'Is it a systematic failure or is it a failure on behalf of some
individuals? I don't know yet but I do intend finding out. What
is very clear to me now is there is a very big difference between
justice and the law,' he said.

In January 2010 Lorcan Roche-Kelly issued legal proceedings
against the State, claiming that McGrath should not have been
granted bail as he posed a significant threat to the public. His
solicitor, Gwen Bowen, confirmed that papers had been issued
in the High Court. Mr Roche-Kelly will argue that the State
acted negligently by granting bail to McGrath. Ms Bowen said
that the case is being taken by Mr Roche-Kelly 'on behalf of the
children as well.'

The case of Jerry McGrath raises many issues about the granting of bail and the sharing of garda information about potentially dangerous offenders. Gardaí invariably check the background of every suspect taken into custody. This is particularly important in any major enquiry, including the investigation into the death of Sylvia Roche-Kelly. Some suspects may have never come onto the radar in the past, while others are known to gardaí. In this case, although McGrath was not known to gardaí in Limerick, he had come to the attention of gardaí in two separate divisions in different parts of the country — Cavan and Tipperary. The senior garda explains, 'We were in contact with the guards down in his locality and by checking our own PULSE [Police Using Leading Systems Effectively] computer system, we would have established the fact that he was out on bail at the time. We became aware, immediately upon identifying him. You had guards in Cavan who were interested in their own case; guards in Tipperary who I would say at the time knew nothing about the Cavan case and then when we came in because it was a murder investigation, we found out immediately about the two cases. If the three cases had happened in Tipperary, or in Limerick, or in the one garda division, where you are dealing with the same individual, certainly the warning signs would go up that here's a guy who attacks a lone female taxi driver and tries to take a child out of a bed; you would be saying this guy needs extra-close marking. An assault on a taxi driver wouldn't be unheard of. The only thing that makes that one more different was the fact that it was a female.

'So, really, if the two of them had happened in the one garda area and the guards there didn't read the signals, you'd be very critical of them. In hindsight, you would look back on this one and say there were a lot of warning signs there. There were a lot of warning signs in Tipperary first day. It depends on your knowledge of the individual, what he has been involved in previously,' the garda says.

Given the seriousness of the offence for which McGrath was arrested in Limerick, he was interviewed in depth by detectives. They concluded that, along with being a dangerous individual, McGrath was also deeply troubled. 'He was very deep, introverted. It was very hard to get into his mind. There were obviously a lot of issues in there. He came from a really, really respectable background. They co-operated with us.' And the garda warns, 'Unless he receives serious treatment in prison, he is going to be a major danger to society when he returns again [after serving his sentence].'

———

While some gardaí who oppose bail in the courts express frustration when bail is granted, those dealing with the investigation into the death of Sylvia Roche-Kelly say it is not a black-and-white issue. Prisons are overcrowded and they are mindful that defendants are innocent until proven otherwise. They say it is simply not possible to remand every single accused person in custody, in advance of trial.

'Sometimes people are critical of judges for granting bail, but there are other times when we ourselves would be critical of our colleagues when they don't object strenuously enough and object to it at a senior enough level,' says the garda I interviewed.

This senior garda believes that judges are doing the best they can and that they take into account the rank of the garda officer who is objecting to bail in a particular case. If an individual's bail application is refused in the district court, he or she then has the option of applying for bail to the High Court. Those applications are made before the High Court on Mondays, where gardaí can voice their objections. The garda recalls one particular case in Limerick where the head of the Limerick garda division, a chief superintendent, opposed bail in a case where a defendant faced a murder charge and the judge accordingly refused bail.

'There was a perception that the particular judge we were appearing before granted bail to everybody. But once the Chief [chief superintendent] went into the witness box and said he believed that further offences would be committed and that it was gangland; the judge took more cognisance of it. It [rank] has to make a difference. Different judges have different interpretations as well. Some are more liberal with bail. Definitely some of it does relate back to the guards and their responsibilities and the level of operation and the rank at which they object to bail. If you have a young guard with one or two years' service objecting to bail for serious charges, what cognisance is going to be taken of that by a High Court judge? Judges are human beings as well and when they see people of a very senior rank, they know there is something more to this; that it's really serious, that it's a cut above the ordinary. There are two sides to every story. You can't say that everybody should be denied bail,' he says.

According to this garda, factors including previous convictions, a likelihood of re-offending, public safety and a risk of interference with witnesses are among those considered by gardaí in opposing bail applications. 'Witness interference would be the main one [reason for objecting to bail] for serious crime. On other more mundane crimes, you would say you know he is going to skip it, or in other cases there you have what we would call a recidivist criminal, someone who just keeps committing crime. If it's going to take twelve months for a case to come up in the district court, how much crime is he going to have committed in the meantime? They are the three main grounds,' the garda explains.

The garda believes that in practice, bail will be granted for most minor charges: 'In fairness to the judges, if the facts of a case aren't outlined and the dangers the State believed someone posed to other people, there is no judge who would refuse bail on [minor] charges, in reality. The reality is, in about a hundred cases, we would only object to bail in maybe nine or ten. There's no reason for us to object to bail in most cases. The ordinary guys who are caught doing break-ins; you charge them. What are you going to object to bail for if they are not a flight risk? We could object to bail on the basis that we have a belief that they are going to commit more crime, but unless they are committing very serious crime, the judges aren't going to listen to us. We'd be firmly of the view that you only go to court in cases where you really want this guy locked up for a very good reason. You do weaken your own credibility with the judges if you are objecting to bail in every case.'

Referring to the bail applications list at the High Court, the garda says, 'If you take the High Court [bail application list] on a Monday, it's frightening. Senior management [senior gardaí, such as the chief superintendent or superintendent] would give out to guards here; they [rank-and-file gardaí] object to bail in the district court. Then they go up to the High Court in Dublin and two barristers will come to them and they will say we have agreed bail on these terms. Those terms could have been agreed in the district court. There is expense involved in taking guards up to the High Court and there is expense in the prison as well. So there is nothing straightforward, from the garda's perspective and from the judge's perspective. It would be very unfair to the judges, and I'm not defending them, to say otherwise. Every case is different and every individual is different.'

According to the garda, practical considerations often come into play when deciding whether or not to grant bail. 'I think judges are very conscious of the fact there is only x amount of prison space as well. The ordinary guards on the street, who are inexperienced, will become frustrated when they don't know the system. But in most cases, the guard should know before the case who is going to get bail and who is not going to get bail. It's not very black and white. There are some cases where people have been granted bail and I would blame the guards. I wouldn't blame the judges. There are other cases I would blame the judges, because they are not listening to it. You just can't lock everybody up, pending the outcome of court cases.'

While gardaí involved in the investigation into the death of Sylvia Roche-Kelly say that it is not all 'black and white', the revelation that McGrath was on bail when he murdered her led to a strong reaction in Limerick, where her family resides. Not only was the entire community deeply shocked that a chance nightclub encounter could end in the death of an innocent woman, but the fact that her killer was on bail provoked a horrified reaction.

Limerick-based TD and former Minister for Justice, Michael Noonan (Fine Gael), spoke out on the issue in February 2009, saying that the bail laws needed to be tightened up. 'The law permits judges to refuse bail to persons who they think will become involved in serious crimes. However, judges are reluctant to refuse bail, as persons are deemed to be innocent until proven guilty and the length of time between the first appearance in court and the trial can be very long; a couple of years in many cases.

'The man who murdered Ms Roche-Kelly was out on bail, and had a history of involvement in violent crime. The fact that he was on bail when he committed this murder has frightened many members of the public, who have justifiable cause for concern,' he said.

'Serious cases involving persons to whom bail is refused should be fast-tracked to take place in months rather than years after an accused is charged,' he added.

Interviewed by me, Mr Noonan says that while the Bail Referendum in 1996 led to change in the terms by which bail would be granted, there appears to be a reluctance to restrict bail. Generally speaking, he believes that while the system should treat everyone fairly, previous track records should be taken into account, when bail applications are made.

'Judges seem to be reluctant to restrict bail, so the expectations of those who proposed the constitutional change have not been realised ... They [defendants] simply shouldn't be let out where there is reason to believe they are likely to re-offend. It is very different, allowing someone out on bail where they have no previous involvement with the criminal justice system, no convictions, and giving bail to someone who has a history of criminal convictions. Of course, the criminal justice system must be fair to all-comers, and each case treated on its own merits, but judges have to take the track record of applicants into account in the granting or refusing of bail,' says Mr Noonan. He also proposes that protocols should be set for the granting of bail, with a view to making the granting of it more restrictive.

Deputy Noonan feels the courts are too lenient in granting bail where serious charges have been brought and believes the current laws do not sufficiently help victims of crime, and in particular where the crimes have been committed by people on bail.

'There is more crime than there was [in the past], especially violent crime, and a significant amount of it is committed by persons on bail,' he says. Mr Noonan believes that overcrowding in the country's prisons is contributing to the problem and is resulting in violent offenders being released on bail, due to a lack of prison space.

———

The Roche-Kelly case prompted a debate on the bail issue, which, fuelled by public anger, lingered on for some time. A Limerick priest also contributed to the debate and spoke of the hurt felt by people who were forced to watch criminals give what he described as 'the two fingers' to the criminal justice system. Speaking to me for this book, Fr Joe Young says that, in general, by granting bail to offenders, the courts are presenting an opportunity for potential witnesses to be intimidated. While gardaí are doing an excellent job fighting crime, they are forced to face numerous obstacles, including the bail laws. He believes that countless families will experience pain, until the bail laws are changed.

'The anger I feel at the moment as a priest — and I believe that anger is an emotional response to perceived injustice — is the fact that I have witnessed too many mothers going through pain. It has caused me great pain and I will never, ever be happy until the bail laws in this country are examined at a serious level. How much more abuse can be given to a mother who has lost her child, an innocent child, and then sitting in the same sitting room where her child may have died, while she looks out the window not knowing where to go and everybody else seems to be free? We have a whole generation of families in this country and it is not going to stop. Futures have been prematurely foreclosed because of a legal system that does not address the fact that when you lose your child, you lose your future,' he says.

Through his work in the Southill area of Limerick, Fr Young has offered support to countless victims of crime. Time and again, he has seen the heartbreak they suffer and firmly believes that the bail laws have played a significant role in all of this. He believes that the freedom available to people out on bail, having committed serious offences, is staggering and the inadequacies in the system have irreparably damaged people's lives. 'It creates what I call the violence of silence because of fear. Fear, fear, fear, in so many of our communities. I don't want to just say it's Limerick. It's right across the board. People are living in fear. And then what is happening is that the people that are suffering as a result of crime are fearful of giving the gardaí what they need. The gardaí are not able to proceed and there is a vacuum there. And, in some way, that has to be dealt with. And I fully respect that you are not guilty until proven guilty. I'm trying to find the balance, but I don't see it.

'The anger among families who have been victims of violence is carried on and breastfed to their children. It's like suicide. There has to be an immediate response. Otherwise, it just goes on and on and on. I don't believe in the blame game but I just feel that society needs to wake up; society in general right across the board, and say, "Enough is enough". We can all make a difference. Freedom in this country is going to be when we all wake up to the fact that we are losing our children to the drug barons and those who can walk out of our courts, having created the greatest hurt in a mother's life in taking her child and just feel it's OK,' he says.

He knows that victims of crime are also deeply hurt by the delays in having cases heard in court. This is very upsetting for victims, who fear that convictions will not be achieved in the courts and that justice will not be done. While it is a defendant's right to have his or her case heard before a judge and jury, Fr Young believes that the slow rate of progress in many cases is a huge problem. 'Why do we have to wait for so long for justice to be served and an impact statement to be made when mothers are suffering right now? They have been given a life sentence. I just feel that it's very hard. Irrespective of whether the crime is solved or not, there is no closure for a mother.'

Chapter 4
A Life Cut Short

Brian Mulvaney was exuberant, energetic and fun-loving. He exuded confidence and was hugely popular among his peers. He had everything to live for; a loving family, a wide circle of friends, a promising future in basketball and a potential career in architecture. According to his mother, Annie, 'He really loved life. He had a big, big personality; one of those guys you would see in a room. He was physically very attractive and a really loud voice and always had something to say. He played music; the guitar. He had loads of friends. Our house was full of his friends. He had a group of about six young guys. They were always together. They played music together. He was very good at basketball. He played with Delta Notre Dame. He was six foot; not extremely tall. We were a very close family.'

Tragically, Brian's dreams were abruptly shattered at the age of just 19, when his life was cut short in a violent incident, just a few miles from his home in Firhouse, Dublin, in March 2000.

Brian was attacked by a group of people, two of whom were later convicted in relation to his death. Brian Willoughby was convicted of murdering Brian Mulvaney, while Stephen Aherne — who was aged 15 on the night of the killing — was convicted of his manslaughter. Willoughby was jailed for life for the murder, while a ten-year jail term was imposed on Aherne for his role in Brian's death. A third man — aged 17 at the time of the killing — also stood trial in connection with the death, but was acquitted.

Brian Willoughby, who was aged 21 at the time of the killing, had suffered from a severe degree of Attention Deficit Hyperactivity Disorder (ADHD) for most of his life. Willoughby was on bail for other offences when he killed Brian Mulvaney. Tragically, Mr Mulvaney met him at a mutual friend's house party in Templeogue on 11 March 2000. At around 1.30 a.m., they both walked from there to a nearby shopping centre. There, they met Aherne and another youth, who had not been at the party. They went to the back of a church to smoke a joint and it was there that Mulvaney was attacked. He managed to break free and ran about 100 yards, but was chased and was caught by the other youth (who was later acquitted at the trial). He was dragged to the ground, where Willoughby jumped on his head, saying, 'This is carnage, boys, this is deadly.' A short time later, Brian Mulvaney was found, in an unconscious state, in the middle of a roadway. His upper clothing had been torn off. He was taken to Tallaght hospital, where he died a short time later.

———

At the trial of the three youths, in March 2003, it was the State's case that all three accused acted together as a gang when they beat Brian to death. The jury was told that Willoughby was jealous of Brian because a girl he was interested in fancied Brian Mulvaney. Most of the people attending the party had been drinking and smoking hash and some, including Brian Mulvaney, had taken ecstasy. According to the State, there was a 'certain territorial aspect' to what had happened, as Brian

Mulvaney was not from that area and there was a fear among some people that he would move in on their territory.

A number of people who had attended the party that night described Brian as being in great form. He was sociable and mixed with other partygoers. The trial heard that in an interview with gardaí, Willoughby admitted asking two others to help him give Brian Mulvaney 'a hiding' but said he was not responsible and had 'just gone berserk'.

In the first statement he made, Willoughby denied any involvement in assaulting Brian, but after his mother urged him to tell the truth, he changed his story. 'I met this guy at the party, I didn't even know his name,' he told gardaí.

'I kept dancing on his head . . . I kept jumping up and down on his head when he was on the ground. I kept kicking and jumping on his head for two minutes . . . then I just left him there. This guy was slagging us off, so I gave him a hiding,' Willoughby told gardaí.

He said he had been on medication for mood swings and depression and that he had smoked hash and had drunk lager on the night of the party. He said he was sorry and that he did not mean to kill Brian. 'I don't feel that I was responsible for what happened, I just went berserk,' he later told gardaí.

The then state pathologist, Dr John Harbison, told the trial that Brian Mulvaney died as a result of injuries sustained in an assault, and not from ecstasy he had taken prior to the incident. However, the defence claimed that the drugs in Brian's system should be taken into account. An independent pathologist, Professor Anthony Busuttil, of the University of Edinburgh — called to give evidence by Stephen Aherne's legal team — said he was unable to rule out the effects of a 'fatal dose' of ecstasy as a contributory factor in Brian's death. He told the court that while Brian had sustained a vicious beating, there were other factors that may have rendered him unconscious. He said that while he did not dispute the cause of death concluded by Dr Harbison, other factors needed to be considered.

Dr Cleo van Velsen, a forensic psychiatrist from the East London Forensic Services, was requested, on behalf of the DPP, to assess Willoughby. She interviewed him at the Central Mental Hospital, Dundrum, in February 2001 and told the jury she did not think that he had a mental illness. 'He had a conduct disorder, which developed into an anti-social personality disorder,' she said. Combined with head injuries he had suffered in a motor cycle accident in 1998, he was very disturbed. 'He suffered from a major abnormality of the mind, not a disease ... Although this is a very disturbed young man, in my opinion at the time he did have the capacity to know what he was doing,' she said.

Willoughby's mother Therese told the trial that her son had cut his wrists and was in a demented and psychotic state days before the killing of Brian Mulvaney, but was refused admission to a psychiatric unit, because there were no beds available. Mrs Willoughby said that on the Monday before the killing, she found her son Brian on the landing of their home covered in blood, having cut both of his wrists. She said he was so aggressive at Tallaght Hospital that it took two security guards to restrain him. However, he was not admitted as there were no beds available. His medication was increased and he was advised to attend an outpatient psychiatric clinic that Thursday.

Therese Willoughby said she reduced his medication, because he was 'so drugged'. He was seen by a consultant registrar on Thursday, but her son was 'worse than ever when I took him home in the car'. The following day, Friday, her son left home in what she described as a 'very demented, aggressive state'. She told the jury that her son was 'totally homophobic' and he felt that anybody that looked at him was a 'homosexual and was going to attack him.'

———

What the court didn't know was that Brian Willoughby had a history of violence. In 1997, a man was walking along College Green in Dublin when Willoughby approached him, asked him if he was gay and repeatedly stabbed him. The man lost an eye as a result of the incident. In 1998, Willoughby carried out a totally unprovoked knife attack on another victim on Baggot Street, Dublin. The victim had to receive a hundred stitches to the body as a result of the attack. Willoughby pleaded guilty to assault causing harm to both men. He also pleaded guilty to assaulting another man on a city-centre bus in Dublin. Willoughby was on bail when he attacked Brian Mulvaney.

At the end of the three-and-a-half week trial, on 2 April 2003, Willoughby was found guilty of murdering Brian, while Stephen Aherne — formerly of Willington Crescent, Templeogue and with an address at College Farm Park, Newbridge, Co. Kildare — was found guilty of manslaughter. The other accused man was acquitted. The jury's verdicts were reached after more than seven hours deliberating. Willoughby was handed the mandatory life sentence, while Aherne was later jailed for ten years.

At Aherne's sentencing hearing, in October 2003, Brian Mulvaney's father, Larry, said that when his son died, 'part of us died with him.' He said his son's head injuries were so bad that he could only identify him through his shoes and hands. 'The system that we live in, there has to be a line in the sand to show that if you cross it, this is what is going to happen to you. How someone could leave someone else to die at the side of the road and not even make a phone call . . . That's pretty hard,' he said. The trial judge, Mr Justice Barry White said, 'A halt must be called to gratuitous violence in our society and a loud and clear message must go out from these courts that it will not be tolerated.'

———

Grief mingled with relief for Brian Mulvaney's family when the trial was over and two men were handed jail sentences. But the court action didn't end there as Willoughby lodged an appeal against his conviction. That was heard at the Court of Criminal Appeal in February 2005, five years after the killing.

In his initial report, the then State Pathologist, Professor John Harbison, had not referred to the presence of ecstasy in Mr Mulvaney's system. Brian's injuries had resulted in the inhalation of blood into the lungs, leading to death by asphyxiation, according to Dr Harbison. At his appeal, lawyers for Willoughby attempted to introduce new medical evidence from a retired pathologist, Professor Dermot Hourihane. Having seen media coverage of the case, Professor Hourihane contacted Willoughby's solicitor after his trial to express concern as to the cause of death of Brian Mulvaney. 'According to the affidavit sworn by the appellant's solicitor in respect of the application now made to this court to admit new or additional evidence, Professor Hourihane intimated to the appellant's solicitor that his experience had taught him that blood in the lungs was a classic symptom when ecstasy poisoning had occurred,' noted the court.

However, the Court of Criminal Appeal stated that the accused's lawyers were aware at the trial of the importance of the issue of the cause of death. They had, according to the court, plenty of time to carry out enquiries as to the possible role played by the ingestion of ecstasy in the cause of death. A first trial had been halted in February 2002 and the Court of Appeal noted that 13 months had passed before the retrial and said this was ample time to research the issue.

The three-judge Court of Criminal Appeal noted that Mr Mulvaney had been the victim of a 'savage assault' on the night of his death. 'It appears that both drink and drugs, including ecstasy, were available at the party. The post-mortem on the deceased carried out by the state pathologist, Professor Harbison, revealed that the deceased had a blood-alcohol reading of 89mg per cent and some small intake of benzodiazepines. The initial report from Professor John Harbison did not refer to the fact that Brian Mulvaney had also consumed ecstasy,' stated the court. 'Professor Harbison noted that the deceased's lungs had accumulated blood and other fluid and concluded that the source of same in the lower lobes of the deceased's lungs was due to the facial injuries sustained by the deceased in the course of the assault. These injuries, particularly in the region of the mouth and nose, resulted, in Professor Harbison's opinion, in the inhalation of blood into the lungs leading to death by asphyxiation. He noted that the deceased's airway, from the tongue downwards to the windpipe or trachea and into the lungs, contained a mixture of blood and mucus. The deceased's cough reflex, which might have enabled him to cough up this blood and fluid, was, in Professor Harbison's opinion, suppressed owing to a concussion which in turn had been caused by multiple head injuries suffered during the assault,' noted the court.

'At no point either during the party, or thereafter until the time of his death, did the deceased evince any signs of illness, diminished consciousness, erratic behaviour or anything untoward or unusual. On the contrary, the evidence in the case demonstrated that his actions both at the party and from the time he left the party were consistent with those of a normal healthy young man of his age. Indeed, on the accused's own account, the deceased endeavoured to escape the assault perpetrated upon him and was later found to have some defensive injuries to his hands and arms. While he was only pronounced dead on arrival at the hospital, it seems clear that his death took place not long after the assault. Following the arrival of the ambulance on the scene, desperate efforts were made to resuscitate the deceased, which included the use of a pump and suction to clear his airways,' noted the Court of Criminal Appeal.

After the jury was discharged in the initial trial, that had opened in February 2002, counsel for the accused in the case were given the opportunity to have remaining blood samples of the deceased analysed. The retrial took place 13 months later. The Court of Criminal Appeal stated, 'In the course of his evidence at the re-trial, Professor Harbison did not alter his view as to the cause of death, notwithstanding the new developments which had occurred. He remained of the view that the deceased died of asphyxiation due to the accumulation of blood/fluid in the lower lobes of his lungs emanating from facial/nasal injuries and which the deceased was unable to cough up, owing to his comatose state attributable to head injuries received in the assault. He described three or four of the impacts to the head as having led to concussion and loss of consciousness. Specifically, he ruled out any suggestion that blood in the lower lobes of the lungs could have been caused by drug overdose.'

The court noted that Professor Hourihane did not appear to have had sight of either the statements or evidence of witnesses who testified as to the behaviour of Brian Mulvaney at the party, or of those who gave accounts of his movements and condition up to, including, and after the assault, or the accounts given by the ambulance team of efforts to clear the deceased's airways. The court refused an application to hear additional evidence.

The court accepted that the particular interpretation given by Professor Hourihane to the pathology and histology findings was not known to the defence legal teams at the time of the trial. However, the court was surprised that they did not have such knowledge. 'In this case, there had been a traumatic and highly publicised trial in February 2002, which collapsed on the very issue of the role played by ecstasy in the matter of the causation of death of Brian Mulvaney. The critical importance of exploring the role, if any, which ecstasy may have played in his death was thus glaringly obvious from February 2002. An interval of some 13 months then elapsed before the retrial took place. On any view, that was ample time within which to research this issue thoroughly, completely and exhaustively. Could the view now expressed by Professor Hourihane have been obtained at time of trial either from him, or some other expert in the field, by the exercise of reasonable diligence and on making full and comprehensive enquiries? In our view, it could,' stated the court.

While the judges stressed that Professor Hourihane acted from 'entirely proper motives' and did so from well-intentioned concern to see that no injustice occurred, the court ruled against the application. 'This is emphatically not a case where the deceased collapsed at a party where ecstasy was in plentiful supply, nor is it a case where at any time prior to the horrific assault which was perpetrated upon the deceased did he evince the slightest sign of being unwell. On the contrary, he was able to walk some distance to a shop, come away from same, endeavour to elude or escape his attackers and put up such resistance as he could, suffering as a result some defensive injuries to his hands and arms.

'The facial injuries suffered by the deceased seem clearly, from the accounts of witnesses, to have resulted in very significant bleeding which, having regard to the position of his body in the aftermath of the assault, could only have resulted in the inhalation of substantial quantities of blood. Professor Harbison has characterised any other fluid in the deceased's lungs as mucus from the nasal cavities and was not, as has already been pointed out, challenged at trial on this opinion. The unfortunate deceased suffered multiple injuries with both lacerations and abrasions to the face and head and nobody either at the trial or since has suggested they were not such as were sufficient to bring about a loss of consciousness, even if they did not involve major fractures to the skull or facial bones,' remarked the Court.

'For Professor Hourihane to be correct, it would require the occurrence of a truly remarkable coincidence, whereby the ecstasy poisoning contended for, or lung haemorrhage caused by ecstasy, occurred at precisely the same time as this vicious assault. The odds against such an event are, we would think, enormous. We do not believe Professor Hourihane's contribution, however well-intentioned, can be seen as sufficiently 'credible' (giving the word its meaning in the particular context) to raise any doubt, yet alone a reasonable doubt, in the minds of the jury as to the cause of death in this case. A remote possibility is not in this regard to be equated with a reasonable doubt,' ruled the court.

———

Willoughby's legal team also argued that the trial judge had failed to adequately direct the jury that even if they found the accused was not insane at the time of the killing, they could nonetheless find that he did not have the necessary intent to found a conviction of murder by reason of his disturbed mental state at the time of the killing. The three-judge court noted that the defence had called evidence from a psychiatrist, Professor Michael Fitzgerald, who had treated Willoughby in the past. He said Willoughby didn't know what he was doing when he attacked Mr Mulvaney. However, Dr Cleo van Velsen told the court she believed he did know what he was doing. 'The jury rejected the case on insanity, by inference at least preferring the evidence of Dr van Velsen (forensic psychiatrist for the State) to that of Professor Fitzgerald,' stated the court.

The appeal court stated it was not satisfied that the trial judge had failed to give an adequate direction to the jury and that during the course of a lengthy charge, the judge had comprehensively explained the ingredients of murder and manslaughter and the requirement to establish intent in the case of the former. 'No requisition as to the adequacy of the charge in relation to intent or on any aspect of the judge's charge was made by or on behalf of the appellant. We are satisfied that the learned trial judge's summing up was more than adequate to meet any requirements of the case and that the medical or psychiatric evidence was spelled out in sufficient detail to allow the jury consider fully the entire issue of intent,' ruled the court.

The other ground of appeal raised on behalf of Willoughby was that there was excessive intervention by the trial judge during the evidence of Professor Fitzgerald. It was submitted that when the trial judge questioned Professor Fitzgerald at the close of cross-examination by the prosecution, that his questions amounted to conducting the case on behalf of the prosecution. However, the Court of Criminal Appeal ruled that the trial judge did not, in fact, do more than what is permissible. That ground of appeal was also rejected and the appeal was dismissed.

———

One of the toughest times of the past decade for Annie Mulvaney and her family was Willoughby's appeal hearing. 'I think, looking back on it, we did not realise how close it went to losing the appeal and maybe have another trial. Around that time we were the lowest our family has ever been,' Annie says. 'We were so fragile. We were so traumatised. I don't know what would have happened if there had been a retrial. Having said that, it is a right all those guys have. We can't do anything about it. I suppose until the appeal is over, you just can't move. Our family was stuck in that trauma for all that time.'

The Mulvaney family has endured immeasurable pain and grief since the death of Brian. He was Larry and Annie Mulvaney's only son and Aoife Mulvaney's only brother. Aoife was two years younger than him and they enjoyed a close relationship. Annie is originally from France but has lived in

Ireland for more than 30 years, while Larry is a native of Crumlin, Dublin. Annie has very fond memories of her only son. She longed for the day when he would pursue his career in architecture and was very proud that he had represented Ireland in basketball, at under-16 level. Yet for all the heartbreak, Annie remains cool, calm and composed as she talks about her son and the circumstances surrounding his tragic death.

'He was nineteen years of age. He was a lovely fella. We were very good friends with his friends. I suppose we were easy-going parents, what you would call cool parents.

'His family was very important to him. We are a very close family. He spent a lot of time in France as well, with my family. From the age of eight, every two years he would go to France on his own. One year it was him, one year it was his sister and that was how they managed to learn the language. He was very Irish. When you come from a mixed family, you pick one nationality and he was Irish in his way of being.

'He had finished his Leaving Certificate and had taken a year out and wanted to do something in architecture. At the time, he only had enough points to do a technician [architecture] course in Kevin Street [Dublin Institute of Technology]. He had applied for that and wanted to travel to France, visiting my family and his cousins. He was only back two or three weeks from his travels in France when he died,' she says.

Annie had great hopes for Brian's future; similar to the aspirations she has for her daughter Aoife. Dealing with his untimely death has been difficult, but as she talks about his short life, she remains resolutely strong. She and her family have had to be strong over the years as they struggled to cope.

'As a mam, I feel it is such a waste. Brian had so much going for him. He was intelligent. He was talented. They took everything from a guy that could have had so much in his life and there's a very sad feeling about that. I can see Brian's friends, what they are achieving in their lives. It is hard. I have no doubt Brian would have been great because he had everything there for him. When you are nineteen, you just see little bits of this; little flashes of that. You don't know what you are going to do with the rest of your life. That's what is really sad. Aoife is on her own as a sibling and that is tough. All our lives have changed so much. Having said that, we are doing very well,' she says.

———

Annie will never forget the moment she was made aware that something awful had happened to Brian. She was in hospital, recovering from surgery, when the bombshell was dropped. It was her husband Larry who had to tell her the worst news she would ever hear. 'I was in hospital that night. I had been in hospital for a week. His sister Aoife was away in a camp with the school for the week. He was at home with his dad. They had come to see me that night. It was a Friday night. I was coming out on the Sunday or the Monday. They went home and they got a takeaway. He got a phone call. There was something going on in the pub. At around nine o'clock or ten o'clock, he went to a local pub. One of the girls that he liked was going to a party. The lads said to him, "We don't really know that group of girls. You like her, so you go." One of the lads gave him a lift to the party and the rest of the lads stayed in the pub and he went on his own.

'He arrived there around eleven. At the party he only knew the girls. He did not know anybody else. He's very bubbly. He wasn't shy so that was no problem for him to fit in. Brian Willoughby was at the party. He liked the same girl that Brian liked. They were seen speaking to each other during the night. At some stage, they went outside to get skins at the shop. Brian smoked dope. When they were at the shop, Brian wanted to get a skin. Brian saw two young fellas who were coming from somewhere. Willoughby lived in that estate and knew them. The fact that Brian got on so well with everybody else and the fact that Willoughby liked that girl, for me, he got him to go outside.

'At the time, Brian was a tall guy. He was a very fit guy and Willoughby would have never managed on his own to attack him so that was why he asked somebody else to help him. Brian tried to get away from them and he was running back towards the party and they ran after him. Brian had a hoodie and the hoodie was pulled to stop him. We used to train together and I could never keep up with Brian, but they caught him,' she says.

Annie talks about her recollection of hearing the dreadful news. 'He had nothing with him because everything was at the party. When the police got there, they were told there was a party nearby. They went to the party. They came to our house. My husband was there. The police asked him would he like to have somebody with him because he was on his own. He called his brother so he went with his brother [to the hospital]. He came with his brother and his wife at seven o'clock [to visit Annie in hospital],' she recalls.

———

Annie was quickly discharged from hospital and she and Larry then had to break the bad news to Aoife. 'After that, we had to tell our daughter. She was in Delphi so that was a big thing. We didn't want to say it to her over the phone. We wanted to say it to her, but her friends started to ring her. One of them said something that she started to think, "Could it be Brian?" We actually had to tell her on the phone,' she says.

Just days after her son died, Annie learned that Willoughby had been on bail at the time.

'We realised it within days. A lot of people came to us saying that Willoughby was a really dangerous person. We would know people from around that area and they would have come to us saying that everybody knew about that guy, that he was dangerous, that he was a difficult person. Then the guards told us that he was out on bail; maybe a week after,' she says.

This deeply angered the Mulvaneys, who, at the time, were trying their best to come to terms with Brian's death. 'Oh yeah, in such a way we felt Brian should be alive. You get to hear people speaking about him [Willoughby] and about his circumstances and about his family. Personally I feel that his family — and I don't want to say something that would bring the two families against each other, I don't want that at all — but I think his family were not capable to help somebody who is a danger to others. If you have somebody like that, then I think that person should be taken out and not to be a danger to society. The way things happened the days previous to him killing Brian, he shouldn't have been left the way he was left. He shouldn't have been left the way he was left on the street that night. He wasn't to be out and his family let him be at the party. There was a denial. To me there was a denial within people around him to see that. When you cannot cope, you have to be strong enough to stand up and say he has hurt people before and I don't want it to happen again, but it did and my son died,' she says.

'Willoughby is a very troubled person. He is a danger to others. You have people who have troubled lives. The one thing I think you cannot attribute to ADHD is the fact that he calculated what he did to Brian. At the party he decided that he was going to hurt Brian. ADHD is something that you cannot control yourself. That day he was at a party where he was probably not liked the way Brian was liked. He knew all the people at the party. Brian was a stranger. He didn't know many people and everybody liked him and he started to say, "Well I'm not going to take that, I'm going to hurt you." He actually started to think about what he was going to do to Brian and he went and he asked people to help him,' she says.

The experience she endured lay behind Annie's decision to get involved in Advic, a support group for families of victims of homicide. Annie co-founded Advic in 2005 and since then has been heavily involved in its work. Advic has sought to bring about changes to the criminal justice system and aims to find a voice for victims. Annie explains, 'What got me involved in that [Advic] was that there was something very, very wrong with the system. Our son died because of it. It took a long time. It took five years [after Brian's death]. After the two trials, there was nothing left of us. The strength was there to get us over the three years. Afterwards we just had to build ourselves up again. We were saying we would not let that destroy us as a family. On many occasions, it was so, so close and we really had to work at that, so, so hard to keep us as a family. Larry and myself were saying we lost our son but we didn't want to lose our daughter and lose the happy family that we had. We were hurting so much. Our daughter was fifteen-and-a-half. She said that she lost her childhood overnight. She lost her innocence overnight,' she says.

Advic plays an important role for families who are affected by homicide. Many of those families feel they have no voice, but Advic aims to ensure they do. 'People that come to us feel that they are understood because everybody there [in Advic] has gone through exactly the same thing, tragically. People feel very comforted by that. Counselling can be very expensive, so we subsidise it, so that is a positive. It has been a big achievement for Advic to have subsidised counselling. In 2007, we started to subsidise counselling. We have subsidised counselling for between eighty to ninety families. That is huge. Most of the people who are members of Advic have gone through counselling and it helps them to recover,' she adds.

———

At its annual general meeting in April 2010, Advic called for legislation to be introduced, which would prevent people accused of murder from applying for bail before their trials. Advic also called for a violent offenders register to be set up, whereby those convicted of crimes of a violent nature would be monitored on their release from prison. Among the other measures it called for included the introduction of murder graded by degree, instead of manslaughter. Advic called for an urgent reform of the bail laws and stated that homicide cases should be dealt with in the courts at a faster rate.

Advic also proposed that the mandatory life sentence for murder be reviewed and that a minimum term of imprisonment of 25 years for first-degree murder be considered. It also suggested that the seven-year parole-application threshold for prisoners serving sentences for murder should be reviewed and consideration should be given to increasing this to 15 years. Parole Board reviews, in cases of murder and manslaughter, should invite written submissions from the families of victims, according to Advic.

———

Annie Mulvaney believes that changes must be implemented and stricter controls should be put in place where bail applications are being made. Had Willoughby been in custody in relation to the other charges he was facing, then her son would never have encountered him on that tragic night.

'Not only did he kill Brian but he has caused other people suffering for the rest of their lives because of his actions. We certainly blame the system for that. The judge should never have given him bail. He should have been sentenced for the crimes that he had committed [in 1997 and 1998]. Unfortunately for Brian, he was in the wrong place at the wrong time,' she says.

Since Brian's death, the bail issue has been debated at length, with various groups and families of victims of crime suggesting different changes that should be introduced. However, Annie

Mulvaney believes that the problem persists and that little has changed.

'I think there is an awareness of the problem, but very little has changed. Judges still give bail every day of the week to people, many of whom are career criminals. Judges don't listen to gardaí who actually work and deal with those people. I know they are trying to work on that, but I think there should be very, very strong legislation. If gardaí or someone very high up in the guards objects to bail, that is something that should be looked at very strongly. There are very, very big issues the number of years' sentence that you get. Those issues are huge. A lot of people suffer from a situation,' she says.

Support groups such as ADVIC face many challenges as they aim to improve the lives of those left behind after homicide.

Annie believes that the current justice system is weighed too heavily in favour of the defendant: 'I would say it is too much in favour of the accused. It should be rebalanced for victims. We are working towards balancing it but there is a long way before it is achieved. There is movement towards it but until such a time, I would be very disappointed by it. You have no choice but to put your faith in it. You have no power. You have no say. The family relies on the State to do something. In France, the practice is that you have some way of taking part but here, you don't and you rely on the State to do that job for you. You have to have faith in it or you have nothing, but I think many, many families are disappointed by it; the fact that the sentences are very lenient; the fact that a person who gets a life sentence is going to be out in twelve or thirteen years; all that means that it is not fair.'

Annie feels that life should mean life. 'If you are sentenced to life, you should serve a minimum of 25 years in prison. The public are the ones that are suffering from it. The criminal justice system has to see that there is a demand for it.'

'I think the criminal justice system is relying too much on the judges. There is not much legislation that they can be guided on, but that should be changed. It's a difficult area. There is legislation for sentencing in relation to crimes involving drugs; maybe [we need] legislation in one sense and also different thinking among judges. I don't think judges meet victims of crime very often. Maybe there should be more relationships like that. At the moment, when do judges meet victims of crime? In the courts. And very often in the courts it is the lawyer that is speaking for victims,' she says.

———

But Annie is adamant that she is not bitter about Brian's death. 'When I think bitterness, I push it away, always. It's a dysfunction. I have never really allowed myself for the bitterness to be very present in my life because it can only destroy you. You can channel your energy into different directions. I generally try to channel it in Advic. Very often when we meet for anniversaries, bitterness would not be part of what we are about. We always try to say what happened happened; Brian died. We can do nothing about that, but we can do something about the future so that the same thing doesn't happen again. I try not to dwell on the bitterness because it doesn't help.

'It is so difficult to keep a family together because everybody is hurting in a different way and we have to accept that. We are a happy family, but we are blessed that we can get on with our lives. We are strong in different ways. We all have strengths and weaknesses. We were always a very open family. We never really lost that, even after Brian died,' she says.

Annie has shown amazing strength and bravery over the years and continues to help families of other victims of homicide. It is difficult to understand how she has maintained that strength, through the unbearable pain of losing her only son.

'You just do it. It was just horrific. He [her husband Larry] suffered really badly. He has suffered a lot over it. He has had nightmares. He was on his own [when the dreadful news was delivered],' she says. Undoubtedly, the nightmares will continue, but it will not hold Annie Mulvaney back from doing her best to ensure changes are brought about to the criminal justice system.

Gerald Barry, who is serving a life sentence for the murder of Swiss student Manuela Riedo in Galway City in October 2007. (*Julien Behal/PA Wire*)

Seventeen-year-old Manuela, with her parents Arlette and Hans-Peter, on holiday just months before her murder. (*Provided by family*)

'Our Angel'. Photos of a smiling Manuela fill every space in her parents' apartment. (*Provided by family*)

Michael Downes, from Ennis, Co. Clare, who is serving a life sentence for the murder of Finbar Dennehy in Clontarf, Dublin, in September 2007. (*Courtpix*)

The apartment complex on Seafield Road in Clontarf, Dublin, where the body of Finbar Dennehy was found. (*Collins Agency*)

Fifty-year-old Finbar Dennehy, a retired executive with Cadbury's, who was murdered by Michael Downes. (*Provided by family*)

Brian Willoughby, who was convicted of the murder of Brian Mulvaney (19), in Dublin in March 2000. (*Courtpix*)

Brian Mulvaney, from Firhouse, Dublin, who was attacked and killed after a party in the south Dublin suburb of Templeogue. Brian Willoughby was later convicted of his murder, while another man was convicted of his manslaughter. (*Collins Agency*)

Brian Mulvaney's parents Larry and Annie and his sister Aoife, speak to the media after Brian Willoughby was convicted of his murder, at the Central Criminal Court, in 2003. (*Collins Agency*)

Mother-of-two Sylvia Roche-Kelly, who was murdered in a hotel bedroom in Limerick city in December 2007. The 33-year-old was murdered by Jerry McGrath (then aged 23) from Tipperary. (*Press 22*)

Michael Doyle, who was convicted of the manslaughter of Marc O'Keeffe in Dublin in May 1997. (*Collins Agency*)

Marc O'Keeffe (20), who was killed by Michael Doyle in broad daylight on a busy playing field close to his home in Tallaght. (*Collins Agency*)

Marc O'Keeffe's parents Thomas and Catherine and his brothers Thomas and Shane, after the sentencing of Michael Doyle. (*Collins Agency*)

Thomas Murray, from Cloonlyon, Ballygar, Co. Galway, who is serving a life sentence for the murder of Nancy Nolan (80) on Valentine's Day 2000. (*Collins Agency*)

Members of Nancy Nolan's family, leaving court after Thomas Murray was sentenced to life in prison for her murder, in December 2000. (*Collins Agency*)

Jonathon Tuohy, of Edward Street, Limerick, who is serving a life sentence for the murder of Noel Carmody in Limerick city in September 2003. (*Collins Agency*)

Darren Wallace, of Assumpta Park, Lee Estate, Limerick, who was also jailed for life for the savage murder of Noel Carmody. (*Collins Agency*)

Forty-two-year-old schoolteacher Noel Carmody, the victim of a frenzied attack in a public park in Limerick city in 2003. (*Press 22*)

David Naughton, who was jailed for six years for dangerous driving causing the deaths of Stacey Haugh (16) and Lorna Mahoney (13) in west Clare on 17 October 2003. (*Collins Agency*)

Stacey Haugh, one of the two teenage girls killed in the road accident near the seaside village of Carrigaholt. (*Press 22*)

A plaque marks the spot where Stacey and Lorna were killed. (*Press 22*)

Joseph Cummins, of St Joseph's Park, Nenagh, Co. Tipperary, who was jailed for 15 years for the rape of a 75-year-old woman in Tipperary in May 2005. (*Collins Agency*)

Anthony Connors, of Tulip Court, Darndale, Dublin, who broke into the homes of several pensioners in Dublin, for which he was jailed for 11 years — one year suspended — in 2009. (*Courtpix*)

Chapter 5
He Died in his Father's Arms

It was 30 May 1997, and Thomas O'Keeffe was relaxing in the sitting room of his family home at Tymonville Road in Tallaght. He worked as a truck driver at the time and was tired after a long trip from Westport in Co. Mayo. He began to nod off on the couch, but his snooze was abruptly interrupted by a knock on the door. A chilling message was delivered: Thomas's son Marc had been involved in an incident on the nearby football field.

Thomas clicked into gear and sped down to the scene. He could see dozens of people gathered in a circle in the field in Tymonville, which was just 300 yards from his family home. Thomas's heart pounded. He was gripped by panic, but fought off the numbness to make his way to the gathering. His son Marc was on the ground in the middle of the group. An unbearably heavy atmosphere prevailed and Thomas knew that something was horribly wrong. He rushed to his son, kneeled down and held him in his arms. Marc's eyes rolled in his head and within minutes, he had died.

Sitting at the kitchen table in his Tallaght home, Thomas recalls that fateful evening.

'I was home here around 4 o'clock. I was on the sofa having a nap. One of the young fellas from the far estate down there ran up and he banged on the door and said that Marc was involved in an accident. I asked him, "Where?" and he said, "Down at the field". I went down to the field. When I saw the crowd, I knew it was serious. I wasn't able to feel my legs. I wasn't able to get out of the car. I finally did find my feet. I made my way from the car on to the part of the field where there was a huge group. It just opened up. I heard someone say, "Here's his father now". Paul [Marc's brother] was there. He had his top on [covering] his head. I said, "Are you all right Marc?" The scalp was down over his ear. He was hit with a knife from behind. It took the whole scalp all the way to his forehead. And then he just went limp. He died,' recalls his father.

It was more than 13 years ago, but tears flow and Thomas's strong voice breaks as he recalls what happened that evening. 'In a matter of minutes, that was the end of it. It was all over. There were loads of people there. It was a beautiful day. There were women with children because it was such a beautiful day and children were playing football. It was a quarter to six in the evening.

'The police arrived. There was a woman guard and she knelt down. She said to blow into his mouth. I didn't know what to do. I was in shock. So I tried it . . . But he was gone. It was too late. He was taken in the ambulance. I got back into the car and I came up here [home]. The hall door was still open. She [Thomas's wife Catherine] said to me, "Don't you come in here and tell me there is anything wrong with my son."' She just freaked out. I brought her down to the hospital [St James's Hospital]. I didn't say Marc had passed at that stage because I wasn't sure. I just felt him going, but I was just clinging to hope. So we went down to the hospital,' recalls Thomas.

The task of having to identify his son's body to a garda at the hospital was particularly painful. 'A detective came down and said, "Are you his father?" I said, "Yes." He said he needed me to make an official identification. I was brought down to the theatre. Marc was sitting up on a bed, half sitting up. His head was all bandaged up. He [the garda] said, "Just take your time". I said, "Yeah, that's Marc, my son". A neighbour was with me. Then we had to go through all the funeral arrangements, looking at brochures for coffins. It's a thing that you never think you are going to have to do with your kids is look at their coffins. We were all still in shock. We still couldn't believe it. I thought it was this awful dream, just trying to wake up because it is not an everyday thing. I thought this couldn't be true. It doesn't register what's going on.'

Marc's killer was a local man called Michael Doyle. Marc did not know him. Doyle was aged 21 at the time and came from nearby Tonduff Close, Greenpark, Greenhills, Tallaght. At the time of Marc's death, he was on bail in connection with a violent assault on a taxi driver in Rathmines, Dublin, the previous December. Doyle claimed that he had gone to get the knives to protect a friend from a hostile mob.

The fact that it all happened so quickly added to the shock for the O'Keeffe family. It seemed as though Marc had gone to the shop just a few minutes when the thunderbolt was delivered to his parents. 'It took seventeen minutes from the time he [Doyle] had the argument and ran off the football field and went to his girlfriend's house to get the knives. He just ran out of the house. Seventeen minutes gave him enough time to cool down as he knew what he was doing, but he didn't. He had enough time to calm down but he didn't do that,' Thomas adds.

Thomas and Catherine O'Keeffe could hardly believe what had happened. To lose a child in such tragic circumstances and so suddenly, such a short distance from their family home, did not bear thinking about. It did not make sense. Marc had planned to go on his first overseas holiday just weeks later, towards the end of June 1997. He and two of his friends were eagerly anticipating their trip to Crete and Marc was anxious that his passport would arrive on time. On the day he was killed, Friday, he asked his mother, Catherine, if his passport had arrived. She reassured him that it would arrive the following week. Marc was buried on Monday and his passport arrived in the post the following morning. That was very difficult for his family, who were numbed with grief at the time.

'He died on Friday. He was buried on the Monday. He was supposed to go on holidays with his boss's son and his mate from Enniscorthy. That [Enniscorthy] was where he was going that night he was killed. As he came out of the shop, this girl called him. That's how he ended up down at the field talking to her. He just went to change his cheque,' recalls Thomas.

———

After his attack on Marc, Michael Doyle fled the jurisdiction. He took a train to Belfast, a ferry to Glasgow and a train to London. However, days later, he handed himself in to gardaí and on 3 June 1997, he was charged with Marc O'Keeffe's murder. There were around a hundred people in the vicinity when the attack occurred and those witnesses were interviewed by gardaí, who investigated the incident. The Book of Evidence in the case was compiled and Doyle went on trial at the Central Criminal Court in October 1999, where he pleaded not guilty to murder.

The trial heard various versions of what had happened that evening. Some witnesses claimed that Marc had approached Doyle with outstretched hands, i.e., in a confrontational manner, a suggestion Marc's family continues to dispute. His family believes that Marc was attacked from behind, in an unprovoked assault. It was the prosecution's case that a row had broken out, during which Doyle had been attacked by youths, who brandished poles and a knife. Marc was not involved in this. Doyle then fled the scene and returned a short time later, armed with kitchen knives, hidden in his clothing. Doyle told gardaí that Marc approached him and he saw him as a threat and stabbed him in the chest. Marc sustained severe injuries as a result of the stabbing. The fatal wound was an injury that pierced the right ventricle of his heart.

The trial heard from several of those who had gone to the football field that evening to play football or to chat with friends. It was a popular place for young people to frequent and nobody had ever expected that a stabbing could take place there. Like his brothers and sister, Marc loved to spend time at the field, which was considered a safe place, so close to hundreds of houses in a built-up area. The shock and horror experienced by many of those who were on the field that evening was recalled to Mr Justice Nicholas Kearns and the jury of seven men and five women at the trial, as memories of what should have been an ordinary Friday evening came tumbling back.

One woman, who lived near the scene of the stabbing, recalled going outside that evening and seeing a group of about 30 people of all ages on the football pitch. She said that there was squabbling and she saw a flash and then Marc O'Keeffe fell to the ground. Another witness recalled seeing Doyle stabbing Marc and told the jury, 'I thought he was throwing punches, they were so vicious.' He said when Doyle approached Marc, he was talking to a girl and was facing away from him. Doyle was carrying what appeared to be two blades when he attacked Marc, the witness told the court. 'I didn't think anyone would be that savage to stab anyone like that. What defensive action can you take when someone's coming at you with two knives?' he said.

One of the gardaí involved in the investigation into the death of Marc told the trial that the accused claimed he had fetched knives to save his friend from a mob. He said Doyle told gardaí that he had been attacked by a gang of around ten youths, one of whom had tried to stab him with a Stanley knife. After he ran away and got the knives, he said he was approached by a man whose arms were outstretched. 'I raised the knives and tried to stop him, but he just kept coming. I raised both my hands with the knives so he could see I had the knives. I stabbed him then. I know I stabbed him,' he told gardaí.

Doyle, who was 22 at the time of the trial, told the court he had stabbed Marc out of panic, after he and his friend had been attacked by a group of youths. He explained that after having several pints in a pub, he and a friend were walking to his girlfriend's house past the football field, when they encountered a gang of youths. He said that he and his friend were surrounded by up to 25 people and he received a blow to the back of the head. 'It set me forward further into the crowd. They had weapons of some sort. Kicks and boots were flying. I came to my knees and then burst through the crowd. I was still dazed after getting whacked. I turned around to see where [his friend] was and was whacked in the face with an iron bar. I couldn't see,' he said.

He said that three people attacked him. He said he escaped and ran to his girlfriend's house and took knives from the kitchen. He put the knives in his clothes so that his girlfriend's mother wouldn't see them. When he returned to the football field, he held up the knives so everybody could see he had them. He said Marc was talking to a woman on the football pitch. 'I didn't know he was part of the crowd until he started running at me,' Doyle told the court. He said the crowd was screaming at Marc to grab him and that was when he came towards him. 'He faced me with his hands out to grab me,' he said.

'I don't remember how I stabbed him, but I stabbed him. It was a mixture of fear and panic. Basically, I was making sure he wasn't going to grab me. I was sort of in shock,' he said. Doyle told gardaí the only reason he stabbed Marc was to save his friend.

In his closing speech to the jury, defence counsel Barry White, Senior Counsel, described the gang of youths who attacked his client as 'hounds baying for blood. If Mr Doyle was coming in here to lie to you, to seek to pull the wool over your eyes, if he wanted to paint the worst picture of the opposition and the best picture of himself, wouldn't he say, "Marc O'Keeffe had already beaten me up"?'. It's a measure of the man and the honesty of the man before you,' Mr White said. He urged the jury to find his client not guilty of murder, but guilty of manslaughter.

In summing up for the prosecution, Eamon Leahy, Senior Counsel, said the jury must consider why Doyle had not run away when he was approached by Marc O'Keeffe. He said if Doyle was simply afraid that Marc was going to catch him, why did he deliver a repeated stabbing? He said Doyle had decided not to leave the pitch until he had inflicted those injuries and the stabbing had all the hallmarks of returning to the pitch to take revenge.

The jury mulled over the evidence and after deliberating for over two hours, returned a unanimous verdict of guilty of manslaughter. Doyle was remanded in custody and in December 1999, he was sentenced to ten years in jail.

In imposing sentence, the trial judge, Mr Justice Kearns, told Doyle he was a 'menace to society.' It was revealed to the court that Doyle had a previous conviction for a vicious assault on a taxi driver, in which he had 'mutilated' the man's face, by biting him several times. In November 1997 Doyle was jailed for seven years for this offence.

———

Taking into account the previous conviction, Mr Justice Kearns said it was 'incredible to believe someone could behave with such savagery.' He said it was an 'extraordinary aspect to the case' that the killing of Mr O'Keeffe took place while the defendant was on bail.

In November 1997, Dublin Circuit Court heard the details of the grotesque attack on the taxi driver in Rathmines, Edward Forde, for which a seven-year jail term was handed down to

Doyle. The sentencing judge described it as 'an attack of an uncontrolled rabid animal', after hearing that Mr Forde sustained multiple bite wounds to his face. Doyle pleaded guilty to attacking Mr Forde, who worked with Radio Link taxis at the time, on 28 December 1996. Doyle was also handed a two-year jail term — to run concurrently — for attacking Vinny Kearns, another taxi driver, on the same date.

The court heard that Mr Forde collected Doyle, along with another man and a woman, in the Rathmines area of Dublin. Doyle sat in the back of the taxi, behind the driver's seat. A garda told the court hearing that the woman asked Mr Forde to take another man, who had got sick, into the taxi. He didn't want to do this and asked the group to get out of his taxi. When he turned around to see if Doyle was getting out, Doyle lunged at him and started to scratch his eyes. Doyle then bit him ten to fifteen times in the face.

Fortunately for the taxi driver, he was rescued by two students who were walking by at the time and noticed the commotion. Doyle managed to flee the scene and got a taxi to his home. However, colleagues of Mr Forde were quickly alerted and, armed with batons and other weapons, they followed Doyle home. It was at his home that Doyle attacked Mr Kearns, one of Mr Forde's colleagues. He lunged at him and bit him, before eventually being subdued and arrested.

Mr Forde declined to be interviewed for this book, but Mr Kearns did speak of the shock he felt on being attacked by Doyle. Mr Kearns was working that night and was one of the first people to witness the horrific facial injuries sustained by Mr Forde.

'I saw a commotion over at a car in Rathmines. I went over. He [Mr Forde] had that many bites on his face, it was like a punishment beating. It was a horrific attack. Even though he was in such a state, he was able to tell me something about a crest on his [Doyle's] jacket. I rang the guards in Rathmines and told them to get a police car to Tallaght. Four other taxis arrived at the same time. A gang of young fellas took off. We took off after them. We had pickaxes, handles, hurleys and sticks. Michael Doyle walked back towards the direction in which we were going down the lane after them. I just grabbed him. I had his two arms up behind his back. He said, "I wasn't in Rathmines". He just bit into my hand. I boxed him as hard as I could with my right hand. I still have a scar on my hand. I managed to hold him, before he ran into his house. The guards arrived,' he tells me.

'I never thought I'd see him again. He scared the living daylights out of me. I've never experienced pure evil as I did with him. I had him on the ground and could see the evil in his eyes . . . Eddie [Mr Forde] is a totally different person. It has had a grave effect on him. It happened for no reason. If he [Doyle] hadn't got bail at the time, Marc O'Keeffe would still be alive. That's the sickening thing about it,' says Mr Kearns.

His unpleasant brush with Michael Doyle will remain with Mr Kearns forever, while Marc O'Keeffe's family will never forget the devastating impact he has had on their lives. Marc's parents, Thomas and Catherine, and their four other sons and one daughter have endured no shortage of grief since Marc was killed. Friday 30 May 1997 should have marked the start of an ordinary, enjoyable June bank holiday weekend. Marc had worked as a carpet fitter with Carpet Store and had finished work early that Friday afternoon. He went home and had a shower, before going to a local shop to change his wages cheque, in anticipation of a good weekend. But tragically, all his hopes and dreams would be shattered on a local football field.

———

The trial was particularly distressing for the O'Keeffe family. They were unfamiliar with the criminal justice system and found the surroundings of the Four Courts very intimidating.

Allied to this, they also had to bear the pain of hearing the details of Marc's killing during the trial, which lasted less than two weeks. The entire process left a very sour taste in their mouths.

'It was very intimidating for the young fellas [the young witnesses who gave evidence], even for us, because it was our first time in a court. We were thrown in there, not knowing where to sit. We were treated like dirt in the place. At one stage I went out to have a smoke and I wasn't allowed back in,' says Thomas.

'Our thoughts at the time, watching this fella every day and his family hugging one another, having to look at us and Marc's brothers and sister arriving into court every day, knowing the loss we had suffered and then having to go through all of this. He had a senior counsel, two junior counsels, a solicitor and a clerk helping him out. They were going through files. All we had was one barrister,' says Thomas.

The trial heard the details of what happened in Tallaght that fateful evening and the events leading up to the death of Marc. Yet, his heartbroken family felt that Marc himself was barely mentioned in the courtroom. 'Marc wasn't the issue. There was nothing to say that Marc had a life, had a girlfriend, had a job, family, parents; there was nothing like that there for him. It was a case file. It was clinical and it was swift. He was hardly even mentioned during the trial,' says Thomas.

'There was no victim impact statement. There was nothing said about Marc or about how Marc's life was. It was all there for him [Doyle],' says Marc's mother, Catherine, who feels that the trial was cold and clinical.

There was plenty of reference, however, to the horrific injuries sustained by Marc in his final moments. While some of the witnesses in the trial claimed that Marc had approached Doyle with his arms outstretched, the O'Keeffe family firmly believe that he was struck from behind and this spun him around to face his killer.

'I was there for the forensics in the court. There were stab marks on the back of Marc's hands, his chest, his arms, where he tried to fend off the attack, but the fatal blow pierced his heart. The first blow came from behind and spun him,' says his father.

Thomas and Catherine and their sons, Thomas, Paul, David and Shane and only daughter Lynda, will never forget Marc. They remember him as being quiet, shy and very hard-working. He enjoyed a great relationship with his employer. Marc worked in Dublin during the week and spent many weekends visiting friends in Wexford. He eventually hoped to set up his own business, in the carpet trade. Brown-haired Marc had a lean physique and loved soccer. He was the first born to Thomas and Catherine O'Keeffe and they adored him. 'Marc was born on 25 January 1977. He was a hard worker. He wanted to set up his own business. He used to go into people's homes, putting down carpets, but he reckoned he was the best at that. He was a normal young fella. He would just go with the flow. He loved football, especially Liverpool. That's on his headstone,' says Thomas, with pride in his voice.

Catherine's memories of her son are of his love of life and his enthusiasm for whatever he did, in his own quiet way. 'He had plans to get a van and go out on his own and do the carpets. Thomas [his younger brother] was meant to do it with him. He was really looking forward to the holiday. It was going to be his first holiday. He was going in June. I said to him, "You never got any shorts or anything". He said, "I'll get them", but he never got them,' she says sadly.

'Marc suffered very badly with hay fever. That day it was a gorgeous day, but it didn't bother him that day. It was strange. When you think of things after, it's really strange. He just walked out the door and that was the last I saw of Marc ... The short life that he had,' she says. According to Catherine, family was very important to Marc and he was particularly close to his brothers Thomas and Paul, who are nearest in age to him.

Thomas was born the year after Marc, while Paul was born the following year. As the eldest in the family, Marc often joked, when his father was not present, that he was the boss!

Each member of the O'Keeffe family has dealt with the death of Marc in his/her own way. Thomas and Catherine are eager to talk about him and they openly discuss his life, his death and the events that followed. As they flick through newspaper cuttings — all of which are stored safely in their home — of the coverage of Marc's death, it all brings back sad memories, but it ensures that Marc is not forgotten. While they have learned, over the years, to cope with the pain, it has not got any easier for them, particularly for Thomas, who clearly remembers the day when all of his dreams for his son were wiped away, in a few short minutes. 'It's like it only happened five minutes ago. I can tell you every detail. It's there in my mind. It's always there,' he says. The fact that Marc was killed so close to their family home means that there are constant reminders. They have considered moving house, to get away from it all, but have concluded that if they move, they will be leaving Marc behind and that is not something they want to do. Although he is no longer with them in person, Marc will always be at the forefront of his parents' minds.

The pain is particularly acute on certain occasions, such as birthdays, Christmas and New Year's Eve. Marc would have been 21 in January 1998, but instead of his family being able to celebrate it with a party, it was marked with a headstone being bought for his grave, while a Mass was said in his memory. It was very difficult for his parents, seeing all of Marc's friends celebrating their 21st birthdays, but their inner strength held them together. The third anniversary of Marc's death was also particularly poignant for his heartbroken family, as his football teammates organised an open-air Mass on the pitch where he was killed. The Liverpool red was to the fore, which was a poignant reminder of Marc's love of the soccer side.

While the O'Keeffes say gardaí were very helpful and

courteous to them in the aftermath of Marc's death, they feel that the system let them down. Several things anger them: from the way they feel they were treated during the trial, to the lack of communication with the authorities, and particularly the fact that Doyle was on bail when he killed Marc. Thomas and Catherine believe that their son would still be alive if the bail laws were tighter. The hurt suffered by the O'Keeffe family on the death of Marc was compounded by this knowledge and will haunt them for the rest of their lives.

'I can't understand why he was out on bail [when he killed Marc]. It's just the way the law is run here. If he hadn't been given bail on the taxi driver, Marc would still be alive. That was a very serious crime that he had done. The guards do all the work and it's out of their hands then. It's the courts that rule then. All the work that they [the gardaí] put in to it and there is nothing they can do,' says Catherine.

When it comes to crimes being committed by people out on bail, the families of various victims of crime point the finger in several different directions. Some say the law needs to be addressed; others blame gardaí; others blame society, while other families blame judges. Thomas O'Keeffe believes that some blame must be apportioned to judges.

'It's down to the system,' he says. 'It's down to the Minister for Justice and the judges. The judges don't live in the real world. They go from their houses, where they would never see any violence or trouble. They only meet upper classes. They never meet ordinary people on the street. I don't think any judge has ever walked down Henry Street or O'Connell Street. I work in the city as a bus driver and I see the drug addicts, the homeless and all that. This can go on and on until the cows come home, but nothing is going to be done. It's the same with knife crime. All our laws are based on Victorian times. Times have moved on a lot in the last hundred years,' he says.

Sadly, he doesn't see any changes emerging, which will better protect the victim. 'I don't have any faith in any changes in the near future or the distant future. The ministers running the country are mixing with the upper echelons, the banks, builders. That's their circle of friends. Anything below that, they don't want to know. They don't want to know about us, yet it's our tax money that is keeping this country going. The system is wrong,' says Thomas.

The entire process was a highly emotional time for Thomas and his anxiety boiled over during Doyle's sentencing hearing, when he shouted across the courtroom, calling him a 'scumbag'. The fury that had built up suddenly erupted. He could see that Doyle would, at the end of his jail term, be a free man, while his son Marc was dead; never to return. The O'Keeffes feel that they were left in the dark on many issues. After being charged in connection with Marc's death, Doyle was granted bail and the O'Keeffes couldn't understand why he had been granted bail a second time. Thomas had plenty of questions, for which he demanded answers. Frustrated by the lack of communication, he decided to visit the office of the Director of Public Prosecutions shortly after his son's death, but left there feeling dejected.

'I wanted to know what was happening. I had never been in this situation before. They wouldn't open the door to me. They spoke to me through an intercom. I was told to go home, that it was none of my business. It was nothing to do with me, it was the State versus Michael Doyle, not me versus Michael Doyle. That's what I was told through an intercom. That was the attitude. That was the start of it and it went on from there, to the courts, to the prisons. They didn't care about us. We had to ask for a meeting with the Prison Service. We were brought to a vacant building. We had to sit with them. One was his liaison officer. The guy that was sitting facing us, he was there for Michael Doyle's welfare. He was getting training and rehabilitation and there would be somewhere for him to go, that his life was on hold at the moment and it would be back on track when he came out. Nobody ever came near us, only the guards. They came here in their own personal time. They were fantastic,' he says.

The family insisted on being kept up-to-date by the Prison Service, in relation to any release that would be granted to Doyle. While this was done, Thomas says that letters from the Prison Service would often arrive at their home on the Monday after Doyle had been on weekend release. 'They were ringing me on Friday afternoon to say he was getting out on Friday morning. So he was already out when they rang me, but I wouldn't get confirmation in writing until the following Monday. I could have been walking down the street and he could have been coming towards me,' Thomas O'Keeffe says.

The dissatisfaction the O'Keeffes felt with the criminal justice system prompted Thomas, like many of the relatives of victims featured in this book, to get involved in setting up Advic (Advocates for Victims of Homicide). Thomas immersed himself in working with Advic, an organisation which has, over the years, raised the issue of the plight of victims of crime and the families they leave behind. Yet, despite all the good work, he doesn't believe that victims will ever have a voice.

'A lot of us got together. We wanted to have a voice for the victim. That is the purpose of Advic. Nobody knew the courts system. Nobody knew what you are entitled to or what you are entitled to have and what happens, what's the procedure, step by step. That was why Advic was formed, to try and organise some kind of sanity into the madness,' says Thomas.

Advic has prepared recommendations on changes to the criminal justice system. While the support group has a sense of optimism that some changes will eventually be brought — which may bring solace to victims of crime and their families — Catherine O'Keeffe finds it difficult to expect much change, in the short-term.

Among Advic's proposals is to have non-jury trials for serious crimes and that previous convictions should be made known to a judge when an individual is charged with a crime.

Catherine believes, 'They are fighting to change all the laws in the bail system. They have to try and get it changed, but it has gone on so long.'

Given that there are so many recidivist criminals in the country, Catherine believes that every bit of information regarding a defendant's previous record should be made available to a judge. 'Oh, yes. The jury is told nothing about them. It's only after he gets sentenced that a jury can read it,' she says.

Her husband agrees. 'Yes. As far as the law goes, murder and manslaughter should be scrapped. There should be the American version, homicide. You take a person's life, it's homicide. The degrees vary on it, on whether it is premeditated or not. A life sentence should mean life. Where does that leave us? Where does that leave Marc? He's forgotten about now. He'll never be seen again on this planet. He'll [Doyle] be out again,' he says. (Michael Doyle was released from prison in January 2009, having served his sentence.)

While the O'Keeffe family fears that Marc's case is simply another statistic in the criminal justice system, he will never be forgotten in his family home and in the minds of the people of Tallaght. Marc's friends wanted him to be remembered in a special way and asked his family to erect a memorial on the pitch where he died. After all, the pitch had been very close to his heart and he had spent many fine evenings there with friends, playing soccer or just enjoying his youth. Thomas and Catherine discussed it with their family and they were receptive to the idea. A granite plaque, with a photograph of Marc and an inscription in his memory, was erected at the end of the pitch, just yards from where he was stabbed. Flowers are regularly placed alongside the plaque and Marc's family and friends often visit, where their fond memories of Marc come flooding back. It is just a stone's throw from the O'Keeffe family home. Thomas frequently goes there, where he has a few words with his son, 'because that was the last place I held him.'

While they are very proud of the memorial and are honoured that Marc was held in such high esteem by his friends, Thomas and Catherine were gutted when the plaque was damaged one Christmas morning. 'Marc's friends asked us to put up a memorial to him in the pitch. They used to sit around that. There was one Christmas morning, it was smashed. It was done by a hammer because Marc's photograph was smashed. We had to get a new one. It was done during the night,' says Catherine.

The O'Keeffe family home is a shrine to Marc, who was a dear son and brother. There are several photographs of him in prominent locations throughout the house, and his parents have held on to all of his belongings. The passage of time has not eased the pain. Thomas O'Keeffe will never get over the moment his son died in his arms. Catherine will never forget the evening that their eldest son died so tragically and so unexpectedly. The emptiness will never go away.

A friend of the O'Keeffe family wrote a song about Marc, the words of which bring tears to his parents' eyes.

A Song For Marc

Let me take you down to that place
I gazed on his face
One final embrace
And he was gone

Sunshine in May was shamed on that day
And taken away
From my precious son

Heart of my life
Now pierced like a knife
It fills me with grief
That I should be here

While you're gone
My lovely son

Or was I only dreaming
I simply do not know
Strange voices in my mind proclaim
That I should let you go
Please tell me that I'm dreaming
For could it ever be
That one as beautiful as you
Should now be lost to me

For such a child of light
Who could be worthy to write
A song for Marc

Let me take you down to that place
Lay flowers on that space
In silence and grace
As we pass on

All life must end
For slayer and slain
But we'll meet again
When tears pass
And sorrow is done
My beloved son

No more I'll spend dreaming
I'll cherish what we had
And even though we're parted now
I know you live in God
And even when I'm dreaming
One thought will comfort me
That one as beautiful as you
Shall live eternally

And in that heavenly choir
Angelic voices inspire
A song for Marc.

Chapter 6
A Shellshocked Community

It was Valentine's Day 2000. Eighty-year-old Nancy Nolan was relaxing at her home near Ballygar, close to the border between Galway and Roscommon.

It was Monday and she had enjoyed the weekend with some of her family. Her sister had visited her the previous day, while two of her six grown-up children had spent time with her over the weekend. She went into the local village of Ballygar at around 12 noon, where she chatted to other locals, before returning home. It would be her final trip to the village.

The retired schoolteacher lived a quiet life, having taught for several years and reared a family. She was a widow, as her husband Tom had died five years earlier. Both she and Tom had taught in the local school, a short distance from their home.

Nancy was highly regarded in the locality, having taught many people in the area over the years. She was remembered as a kind lady, who was generous and caring. Ironically, it was those good-natured attributes that so cruelly cost her her life.

Thomas Murray knew Mrs Nolan. Indeed, they had spoken just weeks before he murdered her. She had taught him in the local school in Ballaghlea many years earlier and he lived just a few short miles from her. The 36-year-old, from nearby

Cloonlyon, Ballygar, was on day release on that fateful Valentine's Day. He was serving a life sentence for the murder of 73-year-old William Mannion 18 years earlier, on 19 July 1981. Mr Mannion, a bachelor farmer from Ballygar, was knifed to death by Murray, who was just 17 years of age at the time. Murray was convicted of murder on 22 February 1982, and jailed for life, at the Central Criminal Court. He was serving the term in Castlerea prison in Co. Roscommon.

While serving the mandatory life sentence, he was granted temporary release on a number of occasions. During one of those temporary releases, he indecently exposed himself to young children in Galway city, in July 1998, for which he was later sentenced to six months in jail.

In the wake of that incident, the temporary release programme for Murray was changed and he was granted day release on a weekly basis. It was during one of those day releases that he killed Nancy Nolan.

————

On the afternoon of 14 February 2000, Murray took a lump hammer from his home and went to Mrs Nolan's house, at Bleannagloos, some three miles from Ballygar, on the Galway road, where she lived alone. Murray launched an unprovoked attack on Nancy Nolan, beating her repeatedly with a hammer, in the hallway of her home. She sustained head trauma, which led to her death. Murray left the scene, hid the lump hammer, and returned to prison that evening, after his 12-hour temporary release. Mrs Nolan's body was not found until the following day, after a concerned neighbour contacted gardaí.

A garda investigation into Nancy's death was quickly mounted and when gardaí became aware that Murray had been on day release on the day of Nancy's murder, he immediately became a suspect. He initially denied involvement, but as the evidence in the case was gathered, gardaí began to believe that he was responsible for the death of Mrs Nolan. After his initial denials to gardaí in March 2000, the following month Murray changed his story and admitted killing her. He informed gardaí of the location of the murder weapon and of his victim's spectacles. The hammer had been discarded in bog water, while the spectacles were thrown into bushes in the locality. Murray was charged with murdering Nancy Nolan and on 5 December 2000, he was sentenced to life in prison, at the Central Criminal Court in Dublin.

Prior to the murder of Mr Mannion, Murray had come to the attention of gardaí on a number of occasions, the first of which was when he was just a teenager. When he was 15, he sent obscene letters to a female neighbour. In 1981, he was charged with unlawfully using language towards her, calculated to cause a breach of the peace. However, the case was struck out when they both agreed to shake hands. Murray was unpopular at school and was believed to have been responsible for puncturing his classmates' bicycle tyres. He finished his primary education, but only attended secondary school for one year, before leaving to work on his father's farm.

Retired Chief Superintendent Bill Fennell, who led the investigation into the death of Nancy Nolan, told me that Murray became a suspect when gardaí became aware that he was on temporary release on the day of her brutal death. Looking back on the case ten years on, Mr Fennell recalls the horrific scene of the murder.

'It was a shocking scene, to go into a house and see a woman lying there in the hallway of her home, just inside the front door. Our investigation swung into action, as was normal. It wasn't until a few days after that that Murray became one of the main suspects and we just happened to get some information that he was seen somewhere near the house at the time. We were carrying out the normal investigations. Every branch of the detective arms of An Garda Síochána was involved in that we had forensics, we had the fingerprints, we had the helicopter and search teams and all there. Eventually we found the murder weapon then in a boghole, within about half-a-mile of her [Nancy Nolan's] house. Murray himself lived within a mile-and-a-half from her,' he recalls.

'He would have been a suspect early on by virtue of his previous history and when we heard that he was around and out that particular day, immediately he became a suspect, because he had committed murder before,' he says.

Gardaí questioned Murray about the murder and when he eventually admitted his involvement, he could not provide a motive. 'At the time, there was no real motive. He had something in his psyche about Nancy. She taught him. He contended that she was a bit hard on him when she was teaching him,' says the retired garda chief superintendent.

It was one of the most horrific cases that Mr Fennell investigated and was not helped by the initial denials from Murray. Asked if Murray was forthcoming in the initial garda interviews, he says, 'No. He was brought in first and interviewed, but it was during the second interview that he admitted it.

'There was more pressure being put on him. We had corroborative evidence. There was a certain amount of forensic evidence as well, but it all essentially corroborated his admissions. It wasn't a case of him planning it for months or anything like that, but it was premeditated because he wouldn't have gone into the house if there wasn't some premeditation of it. What business had he going near the house?'

Looking back on the case, Mr Fennell reflects on the contrasting personalities of Mrs Nolan and Murray. She was much loved and was a pillar of society. He was a loner, a dour and strange young man, who kept very much to himself. 'From our investigations, she was a lady. She went about her own business and went into the town every other day and got her post and did her business and came home and put the car away.

She was a defenceless old lady there on her own. It was a total heinous crime. It was a horrific crime,' he says. Murray on the other hand was, 'dour. That was how I would describe him. He was definitely a loner.'

The murder was cold and callous and left a close-knit community consumed by a wave of shock. The population of approximately 600 people in the rural village had huge difficulty coming to terms with the death of such a respected citizen. They were left baffled and alarmed. Mrs Nolan was fit and agile and cared deeply for those around her. She had always showed a keen interest in her former pupils' progression through life. She was remembered locally as a personable woman. She spoke to everybody in the locality and had always shown a great interest in her roots and in the Irish language. Her son and five daughters were also well-respected people in the locality.

For local people, the pain was magnified when it emerged that Murray was her killer. After Murray had murdered Mr Mannion, many people kept their distance from him, but Mrs Nolan had always treated him well and paid dearly for her kindness. The widespread shock at what had happened to an innocent woman was fuelled further when it emerged that Murray had been on day release from prison at the time. Locals in Ballygar felt that the system had let them down not just once, but twice.

The murder of William Mannion, some two decades earlier, had affected the people of Ballygar deeply. When Murray was charged with that murder just weeks after he carried it out, he told gardaí he had planned that crime but 'not for too long' and said he would not do it again.

Like Nancy Nolan, William Mannion lived alone just a few miles outside Ballygar. He was well-known in the area, having lived there all his life. He didn't know Murray well, but was pleasant to him and when Murray arrived at his home on the evening of 19 July 1981, he had no hesitation in inviting him in for a cup of tea. The two had saluted each other at Mass earlier that day. However, his kind hospitality cost him his life as Murray produced a knife and stabbed him repeatedly — more than a dozen times in total — in the head and neck. Similar to the unprovoked attack on Mrs Nolan, gardaí could not establish a motive for Murray's decision to murder Mr Mannion.

————

The killing of Mrs Nolan immediately led to calls for enquiries to be carried out and clarification was sought on why Murray was allowed out on release, when he presented such a threat. The case featured prominently in the public interest in the months that followed and led to much debate on temporary-release programmes for prisoners serving lengthy sentences. There were concerns that similar attacks could be carried out by other prisoners, if the matter was not investigated and changes implemented. Murray had received various periods of temporary release over a ten-year spell, the final one of which he was on when he murdered Mrs Nolan.

The Department of Justice, Equality and Law Reform pledged to review the case of Murray's temporary release, in an effort to ensure that lessons would be learned in the future. This review would focus on the approach taken in advance of any decisions being made on the temporary release of a prisoner.

Paul Connaughton (Fine Gael) was TD at the time and lives in Mountbellew, Co. Galway, which is close to the scene of the tragedy in Ballygar. He said that the murder of Mrs Nolan had caused anger and upset in the locality and that the Department of Justice had an urgent obligation to review temporary releases of prisoners with convictions of this nature. He raised the matter in Dáil Éireann on 12 December 2000 — just days after Murray was sentenced to life in prison — where much debate surrounded the issue. Mr Connaughton said that the case raised a huge question mark over day releases and he tabled a Dáil question asking the then Minister for Justice, Equality and Law Reform, John O'Donoghue, what steps he intended to take to protect the public — and elderly people in particular — against dangerous criminals who are out of prison, unsupervised, on day release.

In reply, Minister O'Donoghue said that he had ordered a review of the handling of the Murray case, because of the serious consequences of the temporary release granted to him and also because of the huge level of public concern the murder had generated. Minister O'Donoghue outlined that he had appointed John Olden, retired secretary general of the Department of Arts, Culture and the Gaeltacht, to carry out the review. He said that Mr Olden had prior experience of Irish prisons administration and was, at the time, the Irish member on the Council of Europe Committee for the Prevention of Torture and Inhumane Treatment in Custody. The Minister pledged that Mr Olden would review all aspects of the handling of the Murray case — as a matter of urgency — and the results would be made known to the Dáil and to the Nolan family.

'I share the horror of all right-thinking people at this murder and I join all those who have extended their sympathy to the family of the victim in their tragic loss. I readily acknowledge the public's concern that the offender was on temporary release from prison at the time he committed the murder,' said Minister O'Donoghue, in reply to Deputy Connaughton's query.

The minister explained that various criteria were applied in reviewing the cases of life-sentence prisoners for temporary release. These include assessment of the potential risk to the public; the seriousness of the offence committed; the individual's behaviour while in prison; the views of An Garda

Síochána; compassionate grounds, along with recommendations by the Sentence Review Group. 'The process leading up to
recommendations made to the Minister involves consultation
with various individuals and agencies who are best placed to
make an assessment as to the individual's readiness or
otherwise for temporary release, but the overriding concern,
when decisions are being made in individual cases, is the safety
of the public,' stated Mr O'Donoghue.

He told the Dáil that over the years, several serious offenders
had benefited from temporary-release concessions under those
arrangements. At the time — December 2000 — 80 offenders
who had been handed life sentences were on release in the
community. 'The majority of these offenders served between
nine and sixteen years in custody. In practice, all such offenders
were granted renewable temporary release whereby, unless the
conditions of release are breached, there has been no
requirement to return to prison, except to renew the temporary
release at specified intervals. Offenders on renewable temporary
release must be of good behaviour. Other general conditions
include supervision by the Probation and Welfare Service and
reporting at regular intervals to a garda station. Other specific
conditions may be applied to fit individual circumstances.
Temporary release automatically ends if any conditions are
breached. In such an event, the individual concerned can
automatically be returned to custody without warrant or
without any further court proceedings. There are currently six
life-sentenced prisoners in custody who have been recommitted
following their failure to abide by the conditions of their
release. These offenders were initially released between October
1996 and January 2000,' said the Minister.

'In other words, it is unfortunately the case that, despite the
most careful assessment being made in advance, certain
individuals will tend to breach the trust that has been placed in
them and will reoffend, sometimes, as in this case, with serious
and tragic consequences. Other jurisdictions, sadly, have similar

experiences. I should, of course, make the point that I have put a stop to the revolving-door syndrome whereby offenders were released because of a shortage of prison accommodation. Prisoners are not now released for this reason and most of those who are released are released under some form of supervision or reporting arrangements.

'Because of the very serious consequences which arose from the granting of temporary release in this case and the very understandable level of public concern it has generated, it requires and deserves a specific response and I have, therefore, decided to have all aspects of the handling of the case reviewed as a matter of urgency,' he explained.

While the move ensured that the issue would remain in the public domain, Minister O'Donoghue's response was criticised by the family of Mrs Nolan and by Deputy Connaughton. The Nolan family declined to be interviewed for this book, but were vocal at the time. Nancy's sister, Eileen Glynn, told *The Irish Times* in December 2000, that she was not satisfied with the response from the Minister for Justice. 'It seems that a life sentence doesn't mean anything,' Mrs Glynn said. Deputy Connaughton, who had raised the issue in the Dáil, accused the Minister of 'sidestepping the issue' by ordering a review of the circumstances surrounding the decision to grant day release to Murray.

Nevertheless, Mr Olden began to carry out the review and within months, it was made available to the Nolan family and to the members of the Dáil. The review was comprehensive and looked at the entire Murray case in great detail. The report, dated 2 April 2001, pointed to weaknesses in the system and recommended a tightening of procedures for managing life-sentence prisoners.

The report stated that at a local review meeting in late 1998, the governor of Castlerea Prison remarked that Murray would 'kill again,' if he was released. However, Mr Olden said the Governor later gave him a 'verbal assurance' that he had not opposed a temporary release for Murray. The report pointed to a discrepancy between Castlerea Prison records and those of the Prison Service headquarters over what decision had been made in relation to Murray, at a meeting in September 1999. Mr Olden described the 'difference in appreciation' between the two parties as being, 'to say the least, disturbing.'

Mr Olden noted that while in prison, Murray received a lot of attention from the relevant services, in particular from the Probation and Welfare Service. Between 4 August 1998 and 24 February 2000, he had 73 meetings with a probation officer. This included eight meetings each in the months of November 1998 and January 1999. 'It is quite clear from reading the papers and talking to the persons who had dealt with him professionally that, like many other persons who have committed murder, Thomas Murray had a difficult personality and would need a lot of attention before he could be safely released back into the community. On the other hand, the psychiatrists and the chief psychologist who interviewed him during the period of his sentence considered that he was not mentally ill,' stated Mr Olden.

'Having spoken to various persons who were familiar with Thomas Murray's behaviour while in prison, I conclude that he would be generally regarded as being socially inadequate but that on the other hand none of the staff, including the female staff, was afraid of him. In fact, he has never got into any serious trouble in the whole 19 years of his imprisonment so far. Significantly, he appears never to have engaged in violent behaviour while in custody,' added the report.

'The Governor's remark, as recorded in the record of the minutes of the local review meeting on 27 October 1998 that, if released, Thomas Murray would kill again, has to be construed in the light of the fact that the Governor chaired subsequent meetings at which a programme (i) of temporary release for Thomas Murray was discussed and (ii) the Governor's subsequent verbal assurance to me that he was not in opposition to such a programme, but that he had thought at the time that before Thomas Murray was granted continuous temporary release (that is to stay at home), there ought to be a full clinical review of the case.

'In the matters of the developments from mid-October 1999, to the date of the murder of Mrs Nolan, a difference in the appreciation of what had been decided (or not decided) in relation to outings for Murray as between the local prison records and the Departmental (prison headquarters) records is, to say the least, disturbing. I think, however, it is clear that even if Thomas Murray had not been accorded visits home unaccompanied for several days in the period (on the last of which he killed Mrs Nolan), it would appear almost certain that such a programme would have been approved after a relatively short time in any case at departmental level. Looking at the affair now in hindsight, it must be assumed that there would have been a risk to people at any time while he was on release,' said Mr Olden.

Mr Olden pointed out that, in general, it is difficult to predict violence and that on his record as a prisoner, Murray would not have been regarded by the prison authorities as likely to commit an extremely violent attack on a neighbour during an afternoon temporary release in the company of his father.

Mr Olden recommended that steps be taken to assess prisoners in future and also took into account the objections by gardaí to bail being granted to Murray.

'I think that it is safe to say that the gardaí, quite understandably, having regard to their own preoccupations and the views of the population with which they work, are generally opposed to and critical of decisions to release persons in to the community who have committed very serious crimes. My understanding is that it is quite normal for the gardaí to oppose the release of persons who are broadly in the same situation as Thomas Murray. The prison administration, in endeavouring to give effect to the policy of reintegrating people where possible into the community, while taking on board the garda views, must be prepared to take the risk of releasing persons about whose behaviour there must always be some doubt,' said Mr Olden.

He said that in the context of the Murray case, there would have to be a tightening up of procedures for managing life-sentenced prisoners and a general review of the practice in relation to the release of prisoners who have committed violent crimes. However, he said he believed it would be a reversal of policy and a real mistake to take the easy way out and say that no risk would be taken in the future. 'That essentially would be a political decision, but one with serious consequences. The vast majority of persons sentenced to life imprisonment do not seriously offend after release. Prisoners without any hope of early release pose special problems and if the numbers of these prisoners increased because of over cautious policies, very serious incidents within the prisons would become much more likely. Unfortunately, there will always be some prisoners for whom that prospect, punctuated perhaps by periods in the Central Mental Hospital, is unavoidable,' he said.

A report from the deputy governor, dated May 1990, stated that in earlier years, Murray had appeared on several disciplinary reports, mainly for failing to obey orders and that, 'while one could not possibly tolerate that kind of behaviour, he gave an impression that he had genuine psychiatric problems at that stage. On the other hand, when he got a change of employment, he changed immediately and started to show an interest and all the unsettled temperament of the past years seemed to have vanished.' A garda report around this time expressed the view that Murray was 'a person of extremely violent nature and that unless he had changed, his release would constitute a threat to the community.' A probation and welfare officer expressed the view that 'returning home seemed a reasonable long-term plan pending confirmation of local opinion' and that Murray would need a great deal of support and supervision if released.

A meeting of a review group in September 1991 concluded that it would not be safe to release Murray back into the community at that time. A case conference in March 1992 concluded that the resettlement of Murray in the community would require a considerable amount of planning.

An appendix in Mr Olden's report stated, 'According to the report of the meeting, there was already a difference of view in the gardaí; the superintendent in the area recognising and acknowledging that Murray's family are anxious that Murray return home, and that he, the superintendent, does not have a difficulty there but the local sergeant had his reservations. It was also concluded that the resettlement should be over a period of 12 months and the possibility of Mr Murray being placed in the training workshop in Ballinasloe should be explored, in which case accommodation would be obtained for him in Ballinasloe from Monday to Friday.'

Over the months that followed, Murray was granted accompanied outings, including visits home. In December 1992, he was granted temporary release for seven days at Christmas. 'In the submission on file, the reasons cited were length of sentence served, his excellent conduct, his having abided by the conditions of all temporary releases granted to date and this recommendation was made in the light of the quoted opposition of the gardaí to his early release,' stated Mr Olden's report. Then, in March 1995, the recommendation was made that Murray be released on fortnightly renewable temporary release.

Following the incident where Murray indecently exposed himself to children in Galway in July 1998, his temporary release was not renewed. It was at a meeting in Castlerea Prison in September of that year that the governor was quoted as saying he was of the opinion that if released, Murray would kill again.

Nonetheless, a subsequent series of accompanied temporary releases, of a few hours' duration each, were approved on 21

January 1999, for compassionate humanitarian reasons; to visit his mother in hospital as she was critically ill. Murray then received two temporary releases on 27 and 28 January 1999, in the company of a probation and welfare officer, to attend his mother's funeral. A series of monthly temporary releases to his father, accompanied by either a probation and welfare officer or chaplain, were also approved. Those began in late February 1999 and continued up to the middle of October 1999. 'The releases were granted for two reasons, the first being humanitarian, to provide Mr Murray and his father an opportunity to support and console each other following the death of Mrs Murray. The second reason was to encourage Mr Murray in his work with the Probation and Welfare Service in developing positive interpersonal relationships and coping with the problems which full release, if granted, might bring,' stated Seán Aylward, then Director General of the Irish Prison Service, commenting on Olden's report.

At a meeting in Castlerea Prison in May 1999, the extension of the programme of accompanied temporary releases was discussed. Murray was to be granted temporary release to the company of his father from morning to evening, for one day every month. This would be contingent on his father collecting him from the prison in the morning and returning him in the evening. It was agreed that he should be considered for this concession the following September, depending on his progress and conduct in the meantime.

Following a review in September 1999, Murray was granted an a.m.–p.m. temporary release once a week. He would be collected from and returned to the prison by his father. That arrangement commenced on 18 October 1999 and continued up until 14 February 2000 (the date he murdered Nancy Nolan). Between 18 October 1999 and 14 February 2000, Murray availed of temporary release on 20 occasions.

In his observations on the Olden report, Seán Aylward made a commitment that steps would be taken to ensure 'the procedural deficits which occurred in this case do not recur.' Mr Aylward explained that 'quite detailed and close attention' was given to the Murray case from July 1998 when he was returned to prison, following charges of indecent exposure. He explained that Murray didn't receive any further temporary release until the completion of his six-month sentence for this offence.

'I agree with Mr Olden's observation that "the difference in the appreciation of what was decided (or not decided)" at the local review meeting in Castlerea in September, 1999 is disturbing. It represents a serious system failure. At the Minister's request, I have further enquired into this particular issue to seek an explanation,' stated Mr Aylward.

'The Department official at the September meeting, a higher executive officer, did not believe that he had the authority to approve such an extension (and he was totally correct in this belief). He has since reconfirmed that he did ·not convey approval to any enhancement to the programme at the September 1999 meeting but merely recorded that the proposal had not progressed. However, the impression of the governor who presided at the meeting in question was that the proposal to extend the programme was subsequently agreed. The minutes of the meeting prepared by a prison clerk who attended the meeting recorded that decision. These minutes were not forwarded to the Department for agreement subsequent to the meeting.

'I cannot reconcile the two accounts. I also cannot reconcile the differences in the accounts of the official and the governor regarding the outing or outings approved over the telephone in early October. This conflict of record and recollection demonstrates a procedural deficit, which I have acted on. However, I am convinced that, on the basis of information then available and in the prevailing circumstances, had specific approval for the programme extension been directly sought by the Governor from myself or any other authorised officer at HQ level, then it would have been so granted and I have always held to this view,' stated Mr Aylward.

———

While the immediate urgency of the matter centred on the Murray case, the various reports would have relevance for future cases as efforts were made to ensure something like this would never happen again. This was borne in mind in the review of this case. As Seán Aylward said, 'Mr Olden recommended that formal reviews of cases such as Mr Murray's should take place at regular intervals and that the "therapeutic services" should play close attention to these offenders from the very beginning of sentence.

'I have taken steps to ensure that all concerned in the decision-making process are now aware that any progression of a long-term prisoner's programme involving temporary releases must be referred to the Head of Prisons Operations Division at the minimum and that a local review, unless it involves the Head of Operations, cannot approve such changes to a prisoner's sentence management. In addition, all prisoners in the long-term category who are returned to prison due to serious breaches of conditions, must have their cases referred to me and prior to any further release being granted, the Minister must be referred to,' he said.

Mr Aylward said that the system failures which had been exposed in the Murray case have been addressed. However, this did not mean that the implementation of these procedures would have changed the outcome in this case. He remarked how Mr Olden had noted that while in prison, Murray had been examined by a number of psychiatrists, none of whom considered him to be mentally ill, while the psychology service didn't view him as having serious psychological problems. 'I cannot find any explanation for the actions of Thomas Murray on that day, nor indeed can any person dealing with him over the years,' said Mr Aylward.

Murray had committed a 'once-off' impulse-driven offence (the murder of Mr Mannion), albeit with grave consequences, and his case was managed conservatively, according to Aylward. Yet he tragically went on to commit 'an appalling and unprovoked murder when on day release on 14 February 2000. Many lessons have been drawn from this case and they are set out very clearly and fully in Mr Olden's report. It has to be said, however, that even with perfect hindsight and through applying established risk-matrix approaches, Murray's risk profile would not have been flagged as presenting the real possibility he would suddenly commit a cold-blooded murder whilst on a one-day release in the company of a responsible adult.'

Mr Aylward said he agreed 'emphatically' with Mr Olden's observation that it would be a reversal of policy and a real mistake to take the easy way out and say that no risk would be taken in this area in the future. 'Our prisons are increasingly populated by offenders serving long sentences. Should the possibility of early release be ruled out for such offenders, especially lifers, serious issues would arise for our prison system. We would have an increasing proportion of prisoners without prospect of release or hope for the future. The ultimate consequences of such an approach would be considerable,' added Mr Aylward.

Furthermore, the policy of reintegrating long-term prisoners back into the community is consistent with modern penal policy throughout Western Europe, he said, adding that the responsibility of the authorities is to manage any risk to ensure that it is reduced to the level where the safety of the public is protected as much as possible. Of the 80 life-sentenced and long-term prisoners on temporary release at the time of the publication of the reports on the Murray case, 24 had been fully released under agreements relating to the Northern Ireland peace process, while the other 56 were under the supervision of the Probation Service.

The Olden report was detailed and its publication led to the hope that a tragedy similar to the Murray case would never happen again. Looking back on the case more than ten years on, Paul Connaughton feels that careful consideration must be given when temporary release is being considered for a prisoner, particularly somebody convicted of a serious offence like murder. As a local representative in the area, he saw at first hand the fear that was instilled in the people of Ballygar when Murray struck not just the first time (when he killed William Mannion), but also when he murdered Nancy Nolan. 'I sincerely hope that anybody who is a convicted murderer, that it would be almost impossible for them to get parole unless they meet very stringent conditions and assessments. The most difficult category of all should be where a person has murdered once. As the years have passed, we have seen cases where people reoffend. Great care has to be taken that communities are safe,' he says.

————

A decade on, retired Chief Superintendent Bill Fennell remembers the dignity of the Nolan family. In the face of deep anxiety and grief, the family assisted gardaí in any way they could, during the investigation into the death of Nancy. They put their hurt, anger and pain aside to help gardaí, who worked tirelessly in their efforts to comb through every single piece of evidence. It was a meticulous investigation, involving more than 40 gardaí, many of whom were very experienced.

'The one thing I must say is the co-operation from the Nolan family was unbelievable. We had one man [a garda] who was liaising with them and there was a flow of information coming both ways. Of all of the murders, it was the one we had the greatest co-operation in the investigation of the crime. There were lots of emotions,' he says.

The community and the gardaí were baffled by Murray's reasons for killing two innocent people, neither of whom had ever harmed anyone. 'They [locals in Ballygar] weren't blaming the gardaí or anything like that. They appreciated our problems in investigating it. We had our job to do. He had been out on parole but his parole was revoked for committing a further offence, but in their wisdom they saw fit to let him out on day release again. I know it was intended for his ultimate rehabilitation, but he had been in, was let out, misbehaved and was put back in again. But then they let him out on day release. A dog has one bite and if he uses that he is a goner,' Mr Fennell says.

He also feels that, in general, gardaí are frustrated by bail being granted to offenders they believe will strike again, but garda officers can only do their job.

'This is it, but that's the way the law is. If it's to be changed, it's going to have to be a legislative change. Don't forget that the judges in the High Court are governed by the Supreme Court, take for example, Justice Paul Carney. He gets the most gruesome of cases to deal with and he's bound legs and arms with the sentences that he can give out,' Mr Fennell says.

Looking back on his career in An Garda Síochána, during which he worked on a number of murder investigations, Mr Fennell said the previous history of an individual shouldn't be ignored, when it comes to a bail application. 'I wouldn't go so far as to say if a person is charged with murder, that bail should be refused. There are people charged with murder and it's reduced to manslaughter and on one or two occasions, it is reduced to grievous assault. It isn't always necessarily murder. It is a hard one, but I would say if there was any history of violence before, then they should be refused bail,' he says.

'It's [temporary release] all part of the revolving-door syndrome that is there. They say it's part of the rehabilitation to let prisoners back on to the street again on a day-to-day basis under strict supervision. I wonder are they supervised sufficiently when they are out?' he asks.

While the issue of crimes committed by individuals on bail continues to prevail more than ten years after the murder of Nancy Nolan, the man who led the investigation into her death believes that while some things have changed, issues of concern still persist.

'Nowadays, bail is not being given as freely as it used to be. They have built a new prison in Portlaoise. There is far more accommodation in Castlerea. But is prison the answer for a lot? People go in to prison for small offences like failing to pay parking fines, things like that. That needs to be addressed.'

Chapter 7
A Frenzied Attack

Noel Carmody was a model citizen. He was a schoolteacher and active member of Amnesty International. He had been out for a pizza with friends in Limerick city, on a night in September 2003, and was walking home though Arthur's Quay park, when he was the victim of a frenzied attack. The 42-year-old was beaten to death, repeatedly struck with an iron bar and kicked, in the early hours of the morning. He sustained more than 100 injuries and was left lying in a pool of blood. He sustained blows to the head and chest with an iron bar in what was later described by gardaí as a violent, savage death. Along with being viciously beaten to death, he was also robbed.

Mr Carmody, from Ballingarry, Co. Limerick, died at the Mid-Western Regional Hospital in Limerick on the morning of 27 September, just hours after he had been assaulted.

The alarm had been raised shortly after 4.30 a.m. that morning, when an emergency 999 call was made to Henry Street garda station, a short distance away from the scene of the attack, in the heart of Limerick city. The caller stated that a fight was taking place in Arthur's Quay Park. The park is enclosed by metal railings and has five entrances.

A garda patrol car was quickly sent to the scene. However, it was soon diverted to deal with another incident nearby. Within minutes, a second 999 call was made to the garda station and as a result of that, a second patrol car was dispatched to Arthur's Quay Park. There were two gardaí in the car.

One of the gardaí saw a man wearing a grey top striking a man, who was lying on the ground, with a silver-coloured bar. The garda saw a second man in a dark-coloured top crouched over the man on the ground. The other garda saw a man wearing a grey top with a silver bar raised in one hand, standing over a man on the ground. He also saw a man wearing a dark-coloured top crouching over the body.

One garda shouted, 'Stop, gardaí', and both men turned around towards him. The man who was holding the silver bar dropped it to the ground. The two men were arrested and taken to Henry Street garda station for questioning. Jonathon Tuohy (then aged 19) was on bail at the time, having been charged in connection with an alleged hijacking and Darren Wallace (then aged 20) was unlawfully at large at the time, having failed to return to prison following a period of temporary release.

Gardaí observed that Mr Carmody had sustained severe injuries, including wounds to his head. He appeared to be in great distress. His pockets had been turned out and he was not wearing shoes or socks, while the bottoms of his trousers had been pushed up to his calves. He was taken to hospital, but attempts to resuscitate him were unsuccessful and he died at 7.15 a.m.

Tuohy and Wallace were questioned by gardaí at Henry Street garda station throughout that day and within hours, they were charged in connection with Mr Carmody's death. Tuohy, of Edward Street, Limerick, and Wallace, of Assumpta Park, Lee Estate, Limerick, were both charged with assaulting

Mr Carmody, causing him harm, at Arthur's Quay Park, Limerick.

At a special sitting of Limerick District Court on Saturday evening, 27 September, gardaí objected to bail and said there was a fear that the accused might flee the area if they were granted bail. The court was told that it would be alleged by the State that Tuohy was seen by gardaí beating Mr Carmody with an iron bar, while it would also be alleged that Wallace was seen crouched over the injured party when gardaí arrived on the scene.

Tuohy's solicitor said his client was in poor financial circumstances and that there would not be any danger of him fleeing the country, if he was granted bail. Wallace's solicitor said his client would undertake to abide by any bail conditions imposed by the court. However, bail was not granted and the two men were remanded in custody to appear again in court on 1 October. Some weeks later, both men were charged with the murder of Mr Carmody and were returned for trial to the Central Criminal Court, sitting in Limerick, on 14 July 2004. Both accused denied murdering Mr Carmody and also pleaded not guilty to robbing him on the same date.

At the trial, the jury was told that Mr Carmody sustained several blows to the head and chest in an attack. According to medical evidence, the injuries were inflicted with a blunt weapon.

Mr Carmody had suffered a collapsed left lung and multiple lacerations to the scalp and skull, while he had also sustained fractured ribs. A garda who attended the scene of the attack that night told the jury of six men and six women that Mr Carmody was on the ground in a semi-conscious state when gardaí arrived. His face was covered in blood, while there was an iron bar beside him. He made attempts to sit up, but was unable to do so. The trial was told that Mr Carmody's shoes and socks, which had been removed from him, were never recovered by gardaí.

The court heard that when arrested on the night of the attack, Jonathon Tuohy's trousers and runners were blood-stained. A garda told the trial that she saw Tuohy strike Mr Carmody with an iron bar. She gave evidence that when she arrived on the scene of the attack, she saw Wallace crouched over Mr Carmody.

The jury heard details of the garda interviews conducted with the accused men. When asked if he cared that Mr Carmody was dead, Tuohy had replied, 'I don't care if he's dead, because people are dying every day. I don't give a f***, if they don't belong to me.' The court was told that when he was asked if he felt any remorse, Tuohy said he did not. A garda witness told the court that Wallace had a VISA credit-card receipt with Mr Carmody's name on it — dated 26 September 2003 — when he was arrested on 27 September 2003. The receipt was from a pizza restaurant in Limerick city, where Mr Carmody had gone on the night before his death. Wallace was also found in possession of a bus ticket, which gardaí say belonged to the victim. Mr Carmody had bought a return ticket to Rathkeale in Limerick just hours before his death.

It was the State's case that the accused men were engaged in a joint enterprise or had a common design (where two people commit a crime together) in relation to the murder and robbery of Mr Carmody.

While Tuohy admitted hitting Mr Carmody up to 15 times with an iron bar, Wallace claimed that he had not taken any part in the beating. He claimed that he had pulled the bar from Tuohy's hands.

Giving evidence at the trial, Darren Wallace said he and Tuohy went to Arthur's Quay Park in Limerick city on 27 September 2003. On arrival there, they saw two men involved in a sex act in the bushes. He said that one of the men ran away, while the other, Noel Carmody, appeared to have words with Tuohy. Wallace told the jury that Tuohy then got into a rage and started to hit Mr Carmody with an iron bar. Mr Carmody fell to the ground and while Tuohy had the bar over his head, Wallace caught it and threw it on the ground. Wallace said he knew that Mr Carmody was badly injured and while he should have called for the gardaí, he just didn't think to do it. Wallace said he was just looking at Mr Carmody, while he was being beaten. He was shocked and he didn't know what to do, the told the jury. He said that he did not strike Mr Carmody at any stage. Asked to explain how his clothes were splattered with Mr Carmody's blood, he said this must have happened when he took the bar away from Tuohy.

However, under cross-examination, it was put to Wallace that he had participated in attacking Mr Carmody. But he denied striking the victim and said it was Tuohy who had hit him with the iron bar. He said he never touched Mr Carmody. He said that he had grabbed the iron bar from Tuohy and this explained why his fingerprints were found on it, when it was discovered by gardaí at the scene.

While Tuohy initially denied involvement, he later admitted attacking Mr Carmody, but claimed that he had been provoked. The court heard he suffered from Attention Deficit Hyperactivity Disorder (ADHD) and had consumed a considerable amount of alcohol and ecstasy tablets, along with Ritalin — a medication prescribed for the treatment of ADHD — on the night of the killing.

CCTV footage taken in an area leading on to Arthur's Quay Park showed the two defendants carrying what appeared to be long silver metal bars. They were seen walking away from Arthur's Quay Park at around 4.14 a.m. and running back in that direction at 4.18 a.m.

At the end of a six-week trial, the jury decided that both Tuohy and Wallace were guilty of murdering Mr Carmody. The jury reached its unanimous decision on the murder charge, on 16 August 2004. Both accused were also found guilty of robbing Mr Carmody, after the jury had deliberated for three hours.

It had been suggested during the trial that Mr Carmody had

been involved in a sex act with another man. However, in the wake of the jury's findings, a garda told the court gardaí believed that this was not the case.

———

It was during this court hearing that it emerged that Tuohy was on bail at the time of the murder. Tuohy, who had 21 previous convictions, had been charged in connection with a hijacking in Limerick. He faced minor charges in connection with this and had been granted bail, at Limerick District Court, on 17 September 2003. These charges were brought, pending directions from the Director of Public Prosecutions. It was not until two months later — November 2003 — that more serious charges in connection with the hijacking incident were brought.

The court was also told on that occasion that Wallace, who had 20 previous convictions, was unlawfully at large at the time of the murder. He had failed to return to Mountjoy jail, where he was serving a sentence for assault, after being granted temporary release in June 2003.

Mr Justice Paul Carney handed down mandatory life sentences to both Tuohy and Wallace for the murder. He also sentenced them both to seven years in jail for the robbery, with both sentences to run concurrently.

Both accused men exercised their right to appeal the convictions to the Court of Criminal Appeal in Dublin. The appeal took place in November 2006; more than two years after the end of the trial. The Court of Criminal Appeal noted that in evidence at the trial of the two men, it had been clearly established that Mr Carmody had been struck brutally to the head and body on multiple occasions. The judges remarked that the evidence of injuries given by the pathologist had taken up more than 30 pages of transcript and had taken more than an hour to describe. The cause of death was multiple lacerations of the scalp, with bruising and multiple fractures to the skull, and trauma to the underlying brain and multiple fractures of the ribs on the left side, with partial collapse of the left lung and a fracture of the left forearm.

'The applicant, Jonathon Tuohy, while denying any involvement originally, admitted to beating and killing the deceased, his defence at the trial being one of provocation. In furtherance of that defence, he called evidence detailing *inter alia*, a long-standing medical condition, Attention Deficit Hyperactivity Disorder (ADHD) from which he suffered,' noted the court. The court noted that medical evidence at the trial stated that Tuohy's condition was regulated by medication, and that this was a condition that made people prone to impulsive acts, without at the time taking into consideration their impact.

The court noted that Tuohy's defence at the trial was that he went into Arthur's Quay Park with Wallace, where he came across Mr Carmody and another man in the bushes engaging in a sex act. Tuohy claimed that while the other man took flight, Mr Carmody allegedly asked him, 'Do you want one as well?' or words to that effect. 'He said he was enraged and embarrassed by the suggestion and recalled striking the deceased with an iron bar, which he had in his hand, across the head once, but he accepted that he may have struck him several times, as, he contended, he blacked out. Jonathon Tuohy, in evidence, said that his co-accused, Darren Wallace, stopped him beating Mr Carmody by taking the bar from him, at which stage he, Jonathon Tuohy, walked some distance from the scene of the beating to nearby steps whereupon he removed his 'hoodie' top and paused for a while,' stated the court. Tuohy claimed that he then returned to find Wallace with the body and it was at that point that two gardaí arrived at the scene.

Referring to Wallace's evidence to the trial, the Court of Criminal Appeal stated, 'Darren Wallace said in evidence he met Jonathon Tuohy on the evening in question, but had not socialised with him previously. Jonathon Tuohy had taken a long metal bar from a skip, which he had broken in two and they had gone to the park and they were 'messing' with each other. He agreed they left the park and returned again a short time later, both with metal bars (which coincided with the cctv evidence from the area outside the park). When they were returning, he said, after hitting Tuohy once, and Tuohy hitting him once, he, Wallace threw away his iron bar down steps at a pier. It would not appear that there is any cctv video evidence in respect of that event. He says they then saw two men, one the deceased, in the bushes, engaged in a sex act and that the second man ran away, at which stage Mr Carmody spoke to Jonathon Tuohy. Darren Wallace said in evidence he did not hear what was said but that as a result, Jonathon Tuohy hit Mr Carmody with the iron bar several times, using two hands to do so.

'He, Wallace, took the bar, with difficulty, from Jonathon Tuohy and sent him away for a few minutes and that he had then dropped the bar. He did not know what to do with Mr Carmody, whom he knew to be badly injured, and then the gardaí arrived. He denied hitting Mr Carmody at all. Evidence was given that Darren Wallace had both contact and impact blood stains on his clothing and shoes,' stated the three-judge court.

———

The Court of Criminal Appeal assessed the grounds lodged by both Tuohy and Wallace, in their appeals. The first ground in Tuohy's application was an argument that the jury's verdict was perverse. His legal team argued that the jury had failed to give appropriate weight to his history of ADHD; that the jury had not given appropriate consideration to the evidence, which was consistent with the account given by Tuohy, and that the jury had failed to give the benefit of the doubt to Tuohy when there were two accounts of the same event in the evidence of two gardaí (i.e. that one garda had seen a man, wearing a grey top, striking a man who was lying on the ground, with a silver bar, and the other garda saw a man wearing a grey top with a silver bar raised in one hand). Tuohy's legal team argued that one of those accounts was favourable to the prosecution and the other was favourable to him. Tuohy's lawyers also submitted that the jury's findings were against the run of the evidence and that the jury returned its verdict after a relatively short period of deliberation, given the complex legal and factual issues before them.

The Court of Criminal Appeal noted that no complaint had been raised regarding the trial judge's charge to the jury in relation to the issue of provocation, which was the essence of Tuohy's defence. 'It is insufficient for an applicant for leave, merely to contend that his conviction was at odds with some portions of the evidence when the weighing of that evidence, the assessment of witnesses and the determination of guilt or innocence, all fall to the jury itself to determine,' stated the judgment.

'In the present case, firstly, the court finds that there was not merely sufficient, but an abundance of evidence upon which the jury could properly convict the applicant of murder. Secondly, it was a matter for the jury to determine whether the accused's history of Attention Deficit Hyperactivity Disorder was, on the expert evidence, a material factor in the context of the defence of provocation, and the extent of such materiality. It was also a matter for the jury to consider, assess, and draw all appropriate inferences from the evidence adduced as to the circumstances of the death of Mr Carmody,' stated the Court of Criminal Appeal.

The court also stated that if there were inconsistencies between the evidence of two gardaí as to whether Tuohy was actually in the course of assaulting Mr Carmody when they arrived at the scene, that was a matter for the jury to determine. 'Whether one or other members of the gardaí agreed as to the precise position of each of the accused over Mr Carmody's body, whether Jonathon Tuohy had an iron bar in his hand in a half-raised position, or whether a member of the gardaí can remember in which hand he was holding the bar, again these were all matters for the jury,' stated the court's ruling.

The precise sequence of events, in what was described by the Court of Criminal Appeal as 'what must have been a fairly confused situation', was also a matter for the jury. It stated where there were were two different accounts or inconsistencies between the evidence of witnesses, the jury was entitled to prefer the evidence of one witness over that of another and clearly, the jury had done this.

The court also ruled that the medical evidence on the effects of the combination of medication, alcohol and illegal drugs on Tuohy was a matter for the jury. It also ruled that the length of deliberations by the jury was not a matter for the appeal court. It ruled that the decision of the jury was not perverse, nor was it at all unreasonable, or against the weight of the evidence.

The court then turned its attention to the grounds of appeal lodged by lawyers for Darren Wallace. A total of ten grounds were submitted. The first of those was a submission that separate trials should have been ordered, which was sought, but refused, prior to the trial getting under way. It was submitted that Wallace was prejudiced in his defence at the trial as a consequence of statements made by his co-accused against him in the course of interviews with gardaí. However, the court did not hold with him on those points.

The appeal court ruled that the issue of whether separate trials should have been granted was pre-eminently a matter for the trial judge. An application had been made on a date prior to the trial, but no further application was made at the start of the trial. The court ruled that discretion had been properly exercised.

The court then moved on to four grounds, which concerned the admissibility of evidence. 'It is contended firstly that the gardaí on duty at Henry Street garda station adopted a "minimalist view" of their duties in regard to the making of entries in the custody records and to maintaining an inventory on the fruits of the search of Darren Wallace while in custody. It is also alleged that he was not offered breakfast at a proper time, and when it was offered, it was unacceptable because it was not accompanied by a knife and fork, with this omission being the basis for an allegation that the gardaí thereby humiliated him,' noted the court.

The court went on to say it was alleged that a garda had a conversation with Wallace in his cell prior to the interview at 1.32 p.m. and also in a yard while Wallace was having a cigarette, and that he allegedly said to him, 'You should admit to robbing him, that is the only way I can see out for you, admit to robbing him, otherwise you are on your own and you know your mother and your sisters are out there and your mother is roaring crying.'

The Court of Criminal Appeal said it had been suggested that the garda was thereby seeking to induce Wallace into making certain admissions. However, this was denied by the garda, whose version of events was corroborated by other garda witnesses, while the trial judge accepted the garda's evidence in relation to this. 'In the course of his cross-examination by counsel for the prosecution, however, it became clear that even if this had occurred in the manner alleged by Darren Wallace, it had not had any such effect or any effect on him, as the applicant exercised his right to remain silent in large tracts of the interview when he felt minded to do so, and made no admissions. A further allegation was made that the VISA receipt and the bus ticket were not in the possession of Darren Wallace when he was taken into custody and searched, and he asserts that they were not in his pockets, it being the case that the only property he had was what he turned out of his pockets upon being requested to do so. Several garda witnesses gave evidence that these two items had come from his pockets,' remarked the court.

The court noted that the trial judge had found in favour of the prosecution on a range of issues, including the validity of the arrest and detention of Wallace; the fact that a notice of rights was given to him and explained to him in ordinary and simple language; that his entitlement to a solicitor was made known to him; that his interview while in detention was proper; that he was cautioned; that the regulations were adhered to; that he was treated properly; that there were no inducements or threats made to him of the type asserted, and that the search of Darren Wallace was proper.

The court ruled that the trial judge was entitled to make the ruling that he did in relation to the admissibility of evidence.

The next ground on which Wallace's lawyers focused was an allegation that the trial judge had wrongly refused to sever the murder and robbery charges. It had been argued that Wallace had been prejudiced as a result of a failure to sever the count of robbery from that of murder. However, the Court of Criminal Appeal ruled that the trial judge's refusal to sever the two counts was in accordance with 'common sense and reason.'

It was argued on behalf of Wallace that the trial judge had erred in law by failing to charge the jury to the effect that the defence of insanity was open to them in relation to Tuohy. However, the Court of Criminal Appeal did not hold with Wallace on this. 'On this issue, the court has two observations. First, the learned trial judge found and stated in his charge that the question of insanity did not arise in the case. Secondly, it is not appropriate for the second named applicant to contend that the learned trial judge ought to have advised the jury that the first named applicant was potentially insane, since it was not a ground relied on by the first named applicant, there being no evidence given at the trial to support any contention that the first named applicant was in fact legally insane. Such medical evidence concerning ADHD as was adduced related solely to the issue of provocation raised by that applicant,' ruled the court.

The issue of common design was raised by Wallace's legal team, in its appeal grounds, but again the Court of Criminal Appeal did not hold with the applicant in this regard. 'It is submitted that there was a failure on the part of the learned trial judge to direct the jury that they must decide the case in the light of the evidence as to the nature of the common design and as to what was within the contemplation of the parties relative to that common design. In reality, this ground of appeal is related somewhat to the last ground, in that one of the key elements raised by this ground is the nature of the medical condition of the applicant, as well as its treatment, which Mr O'Carroll [Wallace's barrister] suggests should be considered as being close to a form of insanity.

'Mr O'Carroll's submission can be summarised as follows. In the present case there was evidence that Jonathon Tuohy suffered from ADHD, and was prescribed the drug Ritalin for its management and control. The nature of the ADHD condition meant that Jonathon Tuohy was impulsive and had an explosive nature, which could manifest itself suddenly. Jonathon Tuohy had consumed alcohol and illegal drugs and in consequence of the nature of the provocation, he had responded explosively and had gone off on a frolic of his own, to which Darren Wallace had not subscribed.' It was submitted that Wallace did not know that his co-accused suffered from the condition and did not know that the condition could lead to volatility on provocation.

'Mr O'Carroll submits that the events which occurred could not have constituted a common design, and the jury should have been charged accordingly. Counsel for the Director of Public Prosecutions argues that the question of common design applies whether an accused was in the whole of his health or suffering from some medical condition. Darren Wallace was not suffering from any medical condition and was not affected by the condition of Jonathon Tuohy as to what he, Darren Wallace, had agreed or acquiesced in doing. It was at all times open to either accused to argue that the other's actions went outside the scope of the common design. However, the charge to the jury had been exemplary in its clarity in that regard,' stated the court.

The jury, stated the appeal court, was entitled to consider and accept or reject the medical evidence as to the manner in which ADHD may affect an individual, and as to such a person's reactions to situations. The jury was also entitled to accept or reject the contention of provocation raised by Jonathon Tuohy, and that the jury had rejected the case made in that regard. The jury was also entitled to consider what it was that Darren Wallace had agreed to be involved in. The trial judge's charge to the jury, in relation to the issue of common design, was very clear and comprehensive, stated the court. 'The court is satisfied that the charge of the learned trial judge in this case was correct in law and appropriate in the circumstances of the present case and he did not commit any error in principle by not recharging the jury in accordance with the requisition of counsel for Darren Wallace, having properly exercised his discretion not to do so,' ruled the court.

─────

This left one final ground of appeal. On the ninth day of the trial, Darren Wallace had spat at a garda as he was leaving the court. Counsel argued that the judge's findings on this incident should not have been made in the presence of the jury: 'Having found that the incident had occurred as contended for, the learned trial judge left over the matter until the following morning and warned that he would expect certain undertakings to be available from Darren Wallace at that stage, failing which, he indicated what course of action he proposed to adopt. On the morning of day ten, the jury being already in court, the learned trial judge asked if those undertakings as to future conduct were available, at which stage it was submitted by counsel on behalf of Darren Wallace that the matter should be dealt with in the absence of the jury,' stated the court.

'On behalf of Jonathon Tuohy, Mr Nix [Tuohy's barrister] argues that his client, too, was adversely affected by these comments, in that he would in effect be "tarred with the same brush", or would be seen by the jury as being the type of person who would be in the company of someone who would carry out the spitting acts found to have been done, and would thereby be prejudiced before the jury in his defence. Counsel for the Director of Public Prosecutions argues that the complaint could not, in reality, be as contended for. He drew the court's attention to the fact that no application had been made on behalf of Darren Wallace on day ten or later to discharge the jury, which — had it been considered to be as serious a matter as was now contended for in hindsight — would have been the likely application made. Nor was there even a suggestion made in the course of submission or argument that there was or could be any prejudice to Darren Wallace, nor was any application or even any contention made that he could not continue to receive a fair trial, and no requisition was made to give any warning to the jury,' added the court.

The appeal court did not accept that the remarks complained of could reasonably be classified as having interfered with either applicant's right to a fair trial. The matter had been quickly disposed of and was not mentioned again as something that required any further comment.

Having addressed all of the submissions made by the legal teams for both Tuohy and Wallace, the Court of Criminal Appeal refused both applicants leave to appeal. 'Taking all the evidence as a whole, the court concludes that the evidence presented and proved by the Prosecution outlined a picture of guilt in respect of each of the applicants, which was sufficiently convincing for the jury quite properly to have convicted both on all charges, and that no possible miscarriage of justice occurred as a result of the complaint raised on these common grounds,' it stated.

The Court of Criminal Appeal's ruling brought to an end the court proceedings in relation to this case and the gardaí could finally close the case file, more than three years after the killing. Gardaí involved in the investigation into the death of Mr Carmody believe that a number of key factors greatly assisted their work. A garda who was involved in the investigation told me, 'It wasn't very difficult to investigate. Blood from the injured party, found on both suspects, was a positive match. Both were arrested at the scene, while one garda witness observed blows being struck with a bar at the scene. CCTV in the area recorded both suspects with the metal bars in the vicinity of the scene. Wallace had property of the injured party in his possession when he was arrested.

'There were a number of witnesses at the scene who rang 999, but most were intoxicated and did not know the suspects, so they could not identify them. However, as a result of the 999 calls, gardaí attended the scene and garda witnesses were very important as they observed both suspects at the scene,' says the garda.

The attack was particularly vicious, given the multiplicity of injuries sustained by Mr Carmody, who was very badly beaten. There were various versions of what exactly happened in the lead-up to the attack, but gardaí firmly believe it was unprovoked. 'This was an entirely unprovoked incident. Tuohy alleged he was propositioned by the injured party and because of his ADHD, he reacted in an uncontrolled manner. However, this defence was ungrounded. Both men struck the injured party in a frenzied attack, which was entirely unprovoked,' says the garda.

Both suspects were interviewed at length by gardaí and while Tuohy claimed he was provoked, Wallace denied involvement. However, gardaí were satisfied that the strength of the evidence against both accused was sufficient to bring charges. 'Tuohy showed no remorse. He claimed he was provoked. Wallace denied the offence. Wallace and Tuohy are both extremely violent individuals,' the garda says.

It was claimed that Mr Carmody had been engaged in a sex act in the bushes with another man, when Tuohy and Wallace arrived. However, gardaí say this claim was never backed up. 'This was just a suggestion from the defence. All witnesses in the park were interviewed and this allegation was not supported by the investigation,' says the garda.

———

In the aftermath of his brutal killing, family and friends of Mr Carmody remembered him as a man who dedicated his life to helping others. According to gardaí, he was an inoffensive individual, who lived his life in a quiet, orderly manner. He had taught mathematics and economics at second level for many years. Although he was not teaching at the time of his death, he had immersed himself in voluntary and community groups, while he was also a member of Amnesty International. In fact, he had spent most of his adult life showing support for voluntary groups.

A single man, he had lived in Limerick city, where he was described by those acquainted with him as a private man, but who was passionate about his chosen projects. After the jury's verdicts were brought in at the Central Criminal Court sitting in Limerick, Mr Carmody's sister, Maureen, described her brother as decent, sociable and independent and said he did not deserve to die in such a way. She said his character had been vindicated by the verdict.

John Lannon of Amnesty International in Limerick knew Mr Carmody for many years. He says he was regarded very highly among colleagues involved in the organisation.

Mr Carmody was very enthusiastic about campaigning for international human rights. 'Noel was a private guy. He was a passionate kind of guy in that he would always take a strong view on things. He did a lot of years of human rights campaigning with Amnesty.

'I often discussed cases in relation to Amnesty with him. He was an active group member. In Amnesty in Limerick, when it was very active, we would have between forty and fifty people on an email list and eight to ten people would have been active members. Noel would have been quite active in the group [discussions] in relation to issues ranging from violence against women in the Congo to the death penalty. The death penalty would have been one that Noel would have been involved in. Any human rights campaigns that came along, Noel would have been very much involved in; mainly international campaigns,' says Mr Lannon.

'Noel worked on a lot of campaigns. He had been a school-teacher and that was one thing he would often talk about. He made children aware of human-rights issues and what was going on in the world. That was one thing he would have been quite vocal on. He would actually be very forthright with his opposition to human-rights violations and injustices.

'He would have been very anxious to get involved in any campaign that came along. He would never shy away from it. He would have been one of the people you could depend on if you were organising an event. From my experience of Noel, he was always a very trusting kind of character. He might be cynical at a lot of what was going on in the world, but he would have been quite trusting of people.

'We would meet once a month and we would have a drink or two after meetings and Noel would always come along. He would be quite energised and enthusiastic,' Mr Lannon remembers.

Noel Carmody's tragic death shocked those who knew him and the violent nature of it alarmed the people of Limerick. The fact that one of his killers was on bail at the time, in relation to another offence, and that the other was unlawfully at large, made it all the more difficult for people to bear. Many of those close to the victim of this vicious attack believe Mr Carmody would not have met such a cruel death, if more stringent bail laws had been in place at the time. For a man who dedicated much of his life to others, his violent death seems all the more senseless.

Chapter 8
'My Baby Taken From Me'

A few years have passed and Geraldine Mahoney's heart remains shattered by the tragic death of her youngest daughter. The evening of 17 October 2003 started normally when her 13-year-old daughter, Lorna, asked her for money for chips. She willingly gave her some small change, said goodbye to her 'baby' and sat down to watch *Coronation Street*, in the front sitting room of her house in Marian Estate, Kilkee, Co. Clare, at 7.30 p.m. Just hours later, her life would change for ever. Lorna and her 16-year-old friend Stacey Haugh were killed when the car in which they were back-seat passengers veered out of control and hit the sea wall, close to the village of Carrigaholt, eight miles away from their homes. The girls were killed instantly. Karl Haugh, Stacey's 11-year-old brother, was injured, but later made a recovery.

'It was a strange day when you think back on it,' Geraldine recalls. 'I used to go walking most mornings early, before they would go to school. She [Lorna] would be always saying to me to get her up in the morning and she would go walking with me. She would be conscious of the puppy fat or whatever! I called her maybe ten mornings; but not a budge. But that morning, for some reason, she came down the stairs and went out that door at twenty-five past seven. She was a morning person. As we went by the secondary school, I remember thinking, calm down, I like peace in the morning! We were chatting away and we were talking about school and this and that. Everything was fine,' recalls Geraldine.

'She went to school and came home. I never did the dinner until about six o'clock in the evening, but for some strange reason I did it early and we had dinner here, sitting here in the sitting room. She went off then with Stacey. We dropped Deborah [Lorna's sister] off to her friend later on. It was coming on for about half-past seven and I was coming back. I could see a head on the couch. It was Lorna and Stacey. She asked could she have some money. I said how much. She said, "Whatever". That was what she always said. She would never ask for a specific amount. I gave her €2 or something. I can't remember what it was. She said that was plenty for chips. She borrowed my tracksuit top. She asked could she stay out until half-past ten as there was no school the next day. She gave me a kiss and said, "Bye Mum, I love you". That was it. Stacey was standing at the wall. That was about half-past seven, because Corrie [*Coronation Street*] was just starting,' she recalls.

Geraldine sat down in front of the television, in anticipation of an evening of relaxation. But it was not to be. While part of that fateful evening is a haze in her mind, she can still vividly remember other parts of it.

'Myself and David [Geraldine's son] were sitting here. He was going off playing pool. Deborah came in and she said there was a bad accident back in Carrigaholt. She said there were two fire brigades gone out. We had heard them but we didn't think anything. You would hear them from here. She said, "Stacey is in it". The first thing that came into our heads was, Well, Stacey was with Lorna. I was ringing her phone but it was just going straight into voicemail. David said, "If you go upstairs, you will probably find it is in her bedroom, as usual". I was just uneasy,' she says.

Deborah left the house and Geraldine waited for news. She felt anxious and uncomfortable. 'Ten minutes passed and Deborah rang me. She was back in Carrigaholt. She said, "There is a crash". I asked her about Lorna. There was a guard standing beside her. She took the phone from Deborah. I asked her was Lorna in the crash. She said, "I don't know". She [the garda] said, "Where are you?" I said I was in Kilkee.

She said, "Are you coming back?" That was kind of confirming it without confirming it. I said, "How bad is she?" and she said, "They are working on her". She said to be careful coming back. I roared up the stairs and I said, "David, it is them". He said something about whose car it was but we hadn't a clue,' she tells me.

'We went back to Carrigaholt. All you could see was flashing lights. We couldn't get up because it was blocked off. I remember running down a hill. There were loads of people there. You know when you read people's eyes like they are feeling sorry for you. There was just something there. I couldn't explain it, but you just read. I went to a guard and she said I couldn't go near the scene. There were fire brigades there and there was a hearse there too. When I saw that I went, Oh sweet Jesus Christ. Then I saw Bridget, Stacey's mum, and she said to me, "Stacey's dead". Keith [Geraldine's son] turned up. David was back there. We were all there. Karen, my other daughter, was in Limerick at the time. We had to ring her. I rang my ex [Lorna's father] to tell him. We didn't have any answers at that stage, but just a gut feeling that it wasn't good. I couldn't see anything. I don't know how long we were there. I have no idea, but I remember seeing a stretcher and I could see her shoes, her runners,' Geraldine tells me.

Geraldine Mahoney eventually received confirmation that Lorna was dead, but was not allowed to see her at the scene. She was numbed with pain. A wave of shock crept in and she couldn't take everything in. Lorna had been with her just a couple of hours earlier in their family home and now her young life had so abruptly been snatched from her. Geraldine just wanted to hold her in her arms for one last cuddle, but she couldn't even do that. She was told that she couldn't see her until after the autopsy the following day.

'That's what I was told,' she explains. 'At that stage, I had no idea what was going on. I don't remember coming home, but I do remember coming to the house and the house being full at that stage. How they got in, I don't know. I presume I didn't lock the door. I had no idea. I remember just coming in and thinking, Get out of here. I don't want ye here. After that, it was just a long, long night. I wanted to see her. At about six o'clock in the morning, I think I had had enough. They told me she was gone to the Regional Hospital [in Limerick] so I rang the Regional. I don't know who I was speaking to, but she was lovely. She said she would ring me back in about twenty minutes.

'It was Ennis [hospital] that rang me back. She said, "Geraldine, of course you can see your child. You can see your child any time." So why I'd been told that [she couldn't see Lorna's body], I don't know. My sister was here. We eventually got out the door to get to Ennis. Lorna's godmother Niamh, who is from Dublin, had been ringing. She asked did I mind meeting her in Ennis. We got to Ennis. It was good in the sense that I had some visions in my head that she was destroyed, but she wasn't. Her face was just a tiny little one. I looked and I knew straight away that her neck was broken. It was gone all blue where it happened. The only thing was, she didn't suffer. They were taking her then to Limerick. Someone contacted the funeral directors to make arrangements. Somewhere between us, we did. That's the only way to describe it,' she says.

As the Mahoneys prepared to bury little Lorna, there were so many questions for which there did not appear to be answers. How did Lorna happen to be in the car? Who was driving the car? Who owned the car? Where were they going? Sadly, many of those questions remain unanswered, even after the passage of time and that is one thing that continues to haunt Geraldine.

'At this stage, I had no idea whose car [it was]. I had no idea what had gone on. The guards never came to tell us anything. We buried her and Stacey and Karl was in hospital. He was pretty bad,' she says.

Given the nature of the fatal accident, a garda investigation was promptly launched. The driver of the car, a homeless teenager, David Naughton, was questioned by gardaí and was charged in connection with the accident. The families of both girls were trying to cope with the devastating news and were also coming to terms with the fact that a court process was looming.

'The guards rang me and told me he was appearing in court in Ennis. I think it was the Friday after the accident,' says Geraldine. Little did she realise at the time that this would be the first of many appearances in a lengthy court process that would continue over the next few years.

Naughton initially appeared before Ennis District Court on 24 October 2003. He was charged with dangerous driving, driving without insurance and without a driver's licence at Moyarta, Carrigaholt, on 17 October 2003. Bail was refused and he was remanded in custody to appear again in court the following Tuesday 28 October. At Kilkee District Court on that date, Naughton — who was then 16 — was granted bail. He was directed to return to Westside House, a unit for homeless adolescents in Galway, where he had resided prior to the crash.

His solicitor submitted to the court that the charges brought against the boy were summary matters. The court was told that Naughton had been visiting his mother in Kilkee on the day of the crash. Inspector Tom Kennedy, prosecuting, objected to bail. He said that Westside House was not a secure unit and there was no control to prevent the boy from leaving there as he wished. He said gardaí were concerned that the boy would abscond.

However, the court was told that Naughton, who had been referred to Westside House on 25 June 2003, had never been a difficult child and had never been abusive to staff. Bail was granted and Naughton was ordered to appear before Ennis District Court on 7 November.

Naughton failed to appear in court for one of the subsequent remand dates, but was re-arrested and brought back to court. He was remanded to St Patrick's Institution. At his next remand hearing, he pleaded with a judge to be released on bail, claiming he had been assaulted by other inmates. Gardaí objected, but bail was granted. Naughton was warned that he faced being sent back to St Patrick's Institution if he breached his bail conditions a second time. Nonetheless, he absconded again and on this occasion, he fled to the UK. A bench warrant was issued for his arrest in the district court in February 2004, when he failed to appear.

Geraldine recalls, 'After that first appearance in Ennis, it was in Kilkee courthouse. My lads [children] were pretty angry at this stage, as they would be. I was getting a bit anxious about it and I was telling them to be calm. I didn't go into the courthouse that day. I did drive up — I don't know who drove me up — but I stayed in the car. I saw him [Naughton] that day on crutches. I realised then he had been on the bus, the Tuesday before they died. Deborah had an appointment for an x-ray in Ennis. I had given them both a half-day and went over with them. This guy had been on the bus that morning. He obviously must have been around. They weren't talking to him on the bus, but maybe they did know him. I genuinely don't know. He appeared in court that day in Kilkee and he got bail. He appeared again. I went to the court.'

At this later remand hearing, Naughton was not to be seen

and at Ennis courthouse, Geraldine was approached by a journalist, who asked her how she felt that he had absconded. She was dumbfounded. She could not believe that this was happening. Her family had been through weeks of hell at this stage and she was heartbroken that this could happen.

'That was the first I heard of it. I got on to the superintendent and asked how come we weren't informed of anything? They put out a warrant then for his arrest. I don't know how long he was missing for. Then he turned up. He went back into court and was remanded in custody. He was in Kilrush Court. He again applied for bail and he got bail. It was amazing, after he absconding. Because he was under age, up to that I wasn't allowed in to the court cases, but that day, I demanded. I wasn't taking no for an answer. I said, "I'm going in there." I went in anyway and he said that he had been beaten up in St Pat's [St Patrick's Institution], so I presume that was why he got bail. I don't know how long that went on for but again he was gone. At that stage, I was fuming. We wanted to know what happened that night. There were rumours. We heard that girls were screaming back there [in the car] that night. There was a lot of that kind of thing going on. We wanted to know what happened,' she says.

———

Stacey's and Lorna's families were hopeful that the case would be dealt with at the earliest opportunity. Their mothers, as parents, wanted justice to be done and they wanted answers. What led to their daughters being in the back of the car when it crashed, near Carrigaholt? Did their teenage daughters know Naughton? Naughton's disappearance meant that those answers would not be forthcoming, in the short-term at least. They could do nothing more than wait in hope, as there was no sign of Naughton.

'There was a warrant issued again. There was no sign of him. I started traipsing down to the garda station at that stage to see if there was an update. There was no update. They told me at some stage that they were going to apply for a European arrest warrant; that he was gone to England. That process went on for a long, long time. Then one day I got a phone call from a guard. He told me he [Naughton] was after being taken into custody there [in the uk] for something else. He said he would keep me informed. We heard that he was going to appear in court in England on the European arrest warrant. I found out what courthouse in England and myself and Karen flew out that morning. I've a brother who lives there. He took the day off work and we went over to hear the case,' says Geraldine.

After a lengthy process, Naughton was extradited to Ireland and arrived at Shannon Airport in Co. Clare on 25 July 2006 and was brought before Kilrush District Court the following day. The bench warrant, which had been issued on 20 February 2004, was executed and Naughton was remanded in custody to St Patrick's Institution. The charges of dangerous driving, driving without insurance and without a driver's licence were withdrawn by the State and he was charged with dangerous driving causing the deaths of the two young girls.

The Book of Evidence on the charge was served two days later at a sitting of Ennis District Court and Naughton was returned for trial to Ennis Circuit Court.

Three months later, in October 2006, Naughton — who was then aged 19 — pleaded guilty at Ennis Circuit Court and a three-year jail sentence was handed down. At his sentencing hearing, Judge Con Murphy said that Naughton had engaged in a campaign of dangerous driving.

The court heard from Sergeant John Ryan, who said that Naughton had bought a 1984-registered Opel Kadett car for just €60, from an acquaintance in Galway, on the day of the fatal crash. Naughton — who was just one week off his 16th birthday at the time of the crash — told gardaí he had been driving in fields from the age of 12 and this was the third car he had driven. On the evening of the fatal crash, he drove to Kilkee with friends. He was seen 'rallying' around Kilkee at around 7.45 p.m. Shortly before the accident, gardaí received a complaint that Naughton was driving dangerously, at 60 miles per hour, around the car park of the Kilkee Bay Hotel on the Kilrush Road, on the edge of Kilkee town.

Sergeant Ryan said that Naughton met Stacey, Lorna and Stacey's brother Karl at the Loaves and Fishes fast-food outlet in Kilkee shortly after 7.45 p.m. and persuaded them to get into the back seat of his car. Naughton drove the car, while a friend of his was in the passenger seat. Karl Haugh told gardaí that Stacey and Lorna had both asked Naughton to slow down, but he failed to do so. As he drove from Kilkee to Carrigaholt, he hit the sea wall at between 70 and 80 miles per hour.

The court was told that Naughton, with addresses in London and Galway, had overtaken a car 'very aggressively' between Kilkee and Carrigaholt, at a speed of up to 80 miles per hour. He was unable to take the bend and hit the wall in a severe impact at Moyarta, Carrigaholt. The car crossed the road and veered into the ditch on the opposite side of the road.

Naughton told gardaí that he had been travelling at 55 miles per hour and was blinded by the lights of an oncoming car.

Ennis Circuit Court was told that prior to the fatal accident, Naughton had no previous convictions, but that he had since been convicted of a minor offence in the UK.

Naughton's barrister said the boy had not had proper parental supervision from a young age and had been sexually assaulted in the past. Counsel said Naughton, who was born in the UK, had asked him to apologise to the girls' families on his behalf, because he did not have the social skills to do so himself. He said Naughton had absconded while on bail in early 2004 because he could not cope with what had happened.

Geraldine Mahoney told the court, in her victim impact statement, that she believed the girls were coerced into the car that night. She explained how she lost all interest in life in the aftermath of her daughter's death. She described Lorna as a 'bright, bubbly, Mammy's girl, the youngest of five.' Lorna, she said, was 'in love with life. No doubt Mr Naughton coerced Lorna and Stacey into that car. The fear Lorna felt in that car will haunt us for the rest of our lives,' she said. Geraldine then addressed Naughton in the hushed courtroom. 'Lorna and Stacey asked you to slow down but you chose to ignore them. Why?' she asked.

Geraldine explained that she could not understand why Naughton was again granted bail, after he had breached it the first time. 'What puzzled us was that the accused was granted bail for the second time after absconding the first time. We felt abandoned by the legal system,' she added. 'We have gone from a close-knit family to a group of individuals struggling with our grief. We live with the memories because that is all we have left,' she told the court. 'There has been a constant fear I may lose another of my children.'

Stacey's mother Bridget Haugh's victim impact statement was read out, while she sat in the body of the court, at Ennis Courthouse. She explained that when she received a telephone call on the night of 17 October 2003, her 'whole world came to an end'. She recalled attending the scene of the crash, where her daughter Stacey had died, while her son Karl had sustained critical injuries.

'I could not bring myself to go to the mortuary as I felt Karl was going to die, too. I was in a state of shock,' she said. Bridget was torn between burying her 'beautiful, vibrant' daughter and travelling to Dublin to visit her son, who underwent emergency surgery and subsequently survived the crash. The heartbroken mother said she remembered her daughter as a teenage girl who loved music, dressing up, cooking and walking. She said that she had struggled with her life since the tragic accident and had been left facing a life sentence. 'Life has been a struggle since,' she said.

Judge Murphy said the case was 'most harrowing' and was on the 'graver scale' of dangerous driving causing death and had been, 'an accident waiting to happen. There is more than ample evidence that this young man was involved in a campaign of dangerous driving. It wasn't just inadvertence that caused this accident, but a campaign, in effect, of a long stretch of dangerous driving,' said the judge.

———

Geraldine wanted justice and the lengthy process tested her patience. The personal toll was immeasurable. She was keen that the case be heard in the courts. She wanted the driver of the car to be held responsible for his actions and she wanted answers to her questions. There were so many 'whys' in her mind and she dearly wanted to know the entire circumstances behind the crash. Geraldine feels that there are still so many unanswered questions about the night of the crash. 'We still didn't know what happened on the night [of the crash]. He gave his version, but we genuinely don't know. At this stage, from seeing him in court, I figured we weren't going to get much out of him anyway. I know in my heart he was only a kid when it happened. I do know that. It could have been one of my kids that did it. Boys and cars is one of those things. It's a boy thing. But he hadn't one bit of remorse. Not one bit. He never said, "I'm sorry", never.

'I know he didn't go out that night to kill my Lorna. I know he didn't. But just come and tell me what happened. He must regret it. How could anybody have to live with the fact they have taken two lives? OK, his solicitor apologised in the court but that was just so hollow. It didn't mean anything,' she says.

While the guilty plea, at Ennis Circuit Court in October 2006, meant that the families did not have to go through the ordeal of a trial, it also meant that many of their questions still remained unanswered. Given everything that had happened, Geraldine was deeply angered by the outcome of the court case. She had waited and waited for justice to be done, but felt that the three-year sentence was not sufficient. She felt let down by the system. Through her solicitor, she wrote to the Director of Public Prosecutions, requesting that the leniency of the sentence be appealed. She said that Naughton had shown no remorse and had done everything in his power to avoid being caught. The Director of Public Prosecutions did appeal the leniency of the sentence and that appeal was heard at the Court of Criminal Appeal in April 2007.

Geraldine explains, 'He did plead guilty and the judge gave him three years. At this stage, I was absolutely boiling with it. I thought . . . the system . . . She had been dead nearly this length at that time and he walks away with three years. He doesn't seem to have any sense of what he'd done. He doesn't seem to have any sense of how much devastation he had left. I was pretty upset, I must say. Three years. I was boiling. I came home and the lads [her children] were saying to just let it go. I felt, I can't let it go. Maybe I'm evil, that some part of me is evil, but I just can't let it go. I got on to our solicitor. I must have nearly drove him demented. He was really, really good. I asked him could we appeal it. He must have been thinking, is there no stopping this woman? He put a lot of time into it. I was still getting seriously stressed with tears and whatever. We put it together and wrote off to the DPP, telling him why we thought the sentence was too lenient.'

Geraldine Mahoney was keen to be present for the appeal hearing. She travelled to Dublin for the appeal in April 2007, with her son Keith and daughters Deborah and Karen. They experienced mixed emotions on the day. It was difficult for them to take everything in, but they were determined to be present. 'It was good and it was bad. We were all up there. It started and the judges were talking and you are trying to pick, pick, pick what they are actually saying. You are trying to absorb it. For a lot of it, I thought, God I don't think we are going to get anything. I remember when they went off to make their decision. The guard said to me not to go and have a cigarette, because they might only be a few minutes. I needed my nicotine fix! They came back and they all spoke for a few minutes. They doubled it [the sentence]. I'm just glad the judges saw it from our point of view. It could have been anyone's kid who did it, but he didn't have any remorse. He didn't come across as having any sense of the devastation he had caused. There was nothing coming across that he was actually sorry for what had happened. I think the only feeling I got was that he was sorry that he got caught. I personally couldn't stomach that. Maybe I'm judging him wrong. I don't know,' she says.

In the appeal, the Director of Public Prosecutions submitted that the offence was at the higher end of the spectrum, where the maximum sentence was ten years. The three-judge court doubled the sentence from three years to six. The court ruled that the three-year sentence was unduly lenient and that a six-year term, and a ten-year driving ban, was more appropriate. The court took into account that Naughton had ignored pleas to slow down and stated that he had shown no regard for his passengers or other road users.

The Court of Criminal Appeal felt that Naughton had shown little sign of remorse and did not have an appreciation of the consequences of his actions for those who had died. There was nothing to suggest he had learned his lesson. The court took into account Naughton's poor family background, while his young age was also considered by the three judges.

On leaving the Four Courts that afternoon, for the first time, Geraldine felt a sense of calmness. It had been a long journey, one laced with mixed emotions, but finally she felt that her battle was coming to an end. The anger, which had been palpable, would slowly wear away. While she fully accepted that Naughton had not intended to harm anyone on that fateful evening of 17 October 2003, she felt his actions in the aftermath of the tragedy were not acceptable and she found this unbearable.

She uses one word to describe how she felt, in the aftermath of the Court of Criminal Appeal ruling: 'Good. For the first time it was something settled in my system. There was a lot of anger here in this house, a serious amount of anger, which is understandable. We are pretty tight-knit, me and the kids. We were trying to figure out what had happened. They were angry towards him. But I wouldn't have that kind of anger. I didn't have that, but I had a sense that I wanted some kind of justice, but I wanted it the proper way. I will bring it as far as I can bring it, the legal way. I just felt for the first time, we had actually been heard,' she says.

A six-year sentence, she believes, is more appropriate and he would get a quarter of that in remission. 'Yes, he would do four. It would give him a bit of time to think.'

———

It took three-and-a-half years for finality to be achieved, in terms of the court process. Finality is something, however, that will never be attained by the families of the two young girls. As they face each day without Stacey and Lorna, the reminders are constant. Looking back, Geraldine Mahoney feels that she, as Lorna's mother, didn't have any rights and that was deeply troubling for her. The fact that it took so long for the court case to proceed added to the huge stress she experienced.

'I think the rest of the family thought I was obsessed with it. I kept fighting. I used to give interviews for papers, so you would keep it up there. They [her children] were really just sick of it at that stage. I don't know how many times they said to me, "Mam, would you not just give it up at this stage?" I wouldn't. The problem with it was, I wasn't actually the victim. My daughter was. She was dead.

'So, you don't really have any rights. The families don't. We couldn't see the Book of Evidence. We weren't allowed to, under any circumstances. Before the case, we weren't allowed to see any of the statements he had made. You aren't allowed any access to any of that. You don't have any rights. You can't have any legal representation in court if there are any questions you want to ask, because you are not really the victim in the legal sense. You are, but you don't have any rights in the legal system. The only thing you are allowed is the victim impact statement. You get that, but I was also told I had to give it in before I read it out in court, in case there was anything in it. You have no right to ask him anything, as to what happened. I had no right.

'Back there [at the scene of the crash] that night, I had no right to see her [Lorna]. When it happened, I didn't know what had happened, just that there was a car crash. I probably wouldn't have picked it up. We were just in total shock. We weren't thinking straight. If I had a logical mind when I went back there that night, I would have got to see her because I would have been strong enough mentally to put my point across. But you don't have rights and there is no-one there to say to you, "Well, this is your right". We did most of the chasing-up ourselves,' she says.

Geraldine feels that families of victims should have some rights, for the duration of the court process. 'When I went down to the court case [when Naughton was originally charged], he was under age at the time. I wasn't even allowed in. You are relying on the superintendent to tell you what happened, or more likely, a reporter, which doesn't seem right. When it comes to the case, you can't be represented. You can ask this or that and as he pleaded guilty in the end, he wasn't asked anything.

'I just feel you don't have any rights. We will never know what happened that night. The only people who will know what happened that night were in the car. But surely you should have some rights or some legal representation somewhere that you can ask the questions that you want asked and try and get some answers?' she says.

Over the years, she has tried to piece together what she feels happened that evening, after Lorna left her home. She understood that Lorna and Stacey wanted a bag of chips and as far as she was concerned, that was the extent of their plans. 'It seems they met him somewhere, as you do, small town. On the night it happened, they had no plans for anything, bar go up to the chipper for chips. They had no plans other than that, that I was aware of or anybody else was aware of. It seems that what happened was he bought a car that day and drove it down and we genuinely don't know. We never got a version from David Naughton. He never explained.

'I was lucky enough in that our solicitor was brilliant. I couldn't praise him enough. Without that, I wouldn't have known where to turn. It shouldn't go to that. Our whole legal system is crazy. They seem to be bringing in new laws left, right and centre, but are we going back into a dictatorship, I feel, sometimes, with the system that we have? But yet the victims never have rights. We didn't have any rights, left, right or centre,' says Geraldine.

'I'd say I would speak for everyone who has had any kind of tragedy, people want to know what happened. Why did my 13-year-old end up inside in that car? 'Til the day I die, I'll never believe she went into that voluntarily. I did include in my victim impact statement that they were coerced into that car, but I will never get an answer to that. People say kids are kids, but your gut will tell you, you know what your own are capable of and what they are not capable of. I totally believe that, because you know them so well. You do know your kids so well. Especially at that age.

'The victim impact statement was the only moment we had and that is at the discretion of the judge. He can decide whether you can or you can't,' she says. 'It's a crazy system. We were told we could have a victim impact statement, that there was a form we could get, and that was it. You don't get any more help. You are not told what you can and cannot say. You are told it has to be checked and you may not be able to say it,' she adds.

———

Through her experience in this tragic incident, Geraldine Mahoney firmly believes that the bail laws in Ireland need to be overhauled. The decision to grant David Naughton bail led to him absconding and this added to her family's trauma. This deeply hurt her, to the extent that she believes offenders should only get one chance. Although Naughton handed himself in the first time he disappeared while on bail, his decision to flee to the UK on the second occasion added to the trauma for the little girls' families.

'You just wonder how that can happen. OK, I can understand someone getting bail. Everyone is innocent until proven guilty. I totally believe that. But at the same time, if he has absconded once, why did he get bail? Really? He said he got beaten up in jail. But did they have any proof of that? It was his word.

'I think if they get one chance . . . In his case, there was an awful lot of background that would suggest when you look at it, he was in care already in a place where they couldn't stop him from leaving. He had total freedom. But the main thing that really gutted me, that still guts me, is that he was able to buy a car. That same young fella; I couldn't sell him a packet of cigarettes. It's illegal. But he can actually buy a car, which is a lethal weapon, whatever way you look at it. He was fifteen years of age, a couple of weeks off his sixteenth birthday. That doesn't make sense,' she says.

Naughton came to the attention of police in the UK and this ultimately led to him being brought back to Ireland, to face the charge arising out of the crash. Geraldine is relieved that he was caught in the UK, as she wanted some element of closure. 'It's a good thing in a sense, because otherwise they would never have caught him. I know that sounds terrible. If he had apologised, I would have been the one who would have stood up in court and said, "Don't lock him up. He's only a kid." But not with that attitude. I just thought, well, there is no point in giving someone like that a break or a chance.

'If you dwell on it too much, it just destroys you. The other side of it is, I got some sense of justice. Look at how many kids who are killed for whatever reason and there are court cases and nobody ever gets found guilty of it. It is happening left, right and centre. And the families have to look at who did it, day in, day out. That must be absolutely horrendous,' she says.

———

Given that the court process has been finalised, Geraldine wants nothing more than for her family to move on. She is determined to live her life as best she can. She never wants to see David Naughton again. 'I don't want to catch a hold of him. I would prefer not to see him. I've done the best that I can do within our system. I can't do any more than that. I don't hold anything against him. Lorna wouldn't want that. She wouldn't look for vengeance. She wasn't the type. At the same time, I don't want him in my face,' she says.

Over the years, Geraldine has experienced good days, but there have also been extremely painful bad days. 'People say with time you will get over it, but it's my view that while you get more used to carrying it, you don't get over it. When it happens, you fall apart mentally and physically and every way and you try to rebuild it, but there is always something missing, like at Christmas, or sometimes there is always a chair that is empty. You cannot fill the chair, no matter what.

'It's just hard; hard to get through things like that. It's her birthday on the fourth of July. Karen [one of Geraldine's other daughters] got married two years ago. I remember going into the shop where she had picked out her dress with the bridesmaids. She was trying on the dress again. Of course she [Lorna] is in your thoughts. We were saying, imagine trying to get Lorna into a bridesmaid's dress. We were laughing, because she was a pure tomboy! Tracksuit and runners and that was it. One minute we were all giggling and the next minute we were all crying.'

Lorna was in second year in Kilkee Community School and had aspired to become a vet. She was a bubbly young lady and, given that she was the youngest of three girls and two boys, she was her mother's angel. Mother and daughter shared a close bond, and that made her death all the more painful. Geraldine regularly refers to Lorna as 'our baby'.

'Lorna was full of life, a real bubbly, bouncy kind of person, full of fun. She hated going into the bath! You would literally have to lock the door. She was always out and about, playing ball or chasing cats and dogs. She was a mad animal fanatic. She always wanted to be a vet's nurse. Then when she went into secondary school and realised that she was bright enough to be a vet, that was the plan. When she was right, she was right. She had a very strong personality. She got on with everybody. She just had that knack. She had everything ahead of her. She was one of those people who would have managed in life.

'She had been to one school disco; herself and Stacey. I had let her go that night. They got the bus to Quilty and Deborah, her older sister, had gone up to keep an eye on her and so had Keith and so had David [Lorna's brothers]. I met them off the bus at about one-thirty and asked her had she a good time. She said, "Yeah, grand". She said to me, "Now, Mam, they didn't all have to come to keep an eye on me. I'm able to look after myself!" She was always very mature. Maybe it was because I was on my own with them and I suppose they had to have more responsibility. Everyone would consider her a totally contented thirteen-year-old. She was just beginning to notice the boys! A few times I had actually saw a bit of eye shadow, you know, normal! She was my little girl. She was the baby. She was Mammy's girl,' she remembers.

—

For Geraldine Mahoney and Bridget Haugh, the heartbreak will never ease. As Geraldine explains, 'You just have to cope as best you can. You have good days. You have bad days. You have brutal days. I think it is one of the worst things that can ever happen to anybody. It is the worst thing that ever happened to me, ever. You genuinely wouldn't wish it on your worst enemy.'

Chapter 9
A Vicious Rape

It was an horrific attack on an innocent woman and had a devastating impact on her. A 74-year-old widow was forced to go through a harrowing ordeal at the hands of a young man, who viciously raped her and robbed her in her Co. Tipperary home in the middle of the night.

What happened to the defenceless woman — who cannot be named, for legal reasons — in the early hours of 22 May 2005, is to most people, totally unimaginable. She had understandably felt safe in her own home and was enjoying the later years of her life, having reared her family and having become a grandmother. On that night, however, much of what she had cherished about life was suddenly snatched from her. Gone was her independence and her security; only to be replaced by cramps of fear and anxiety. The woman no longer felt safe in her home and never returned there, after the attack.

———

The alarm was raised at around 3.40 a.m. on 22 May 2005, when gardaí and the emergency services were called to a house in

Tipperary. On arrival there, they found the victim in a distraught state. As word quickly began to flow around the area about what had happened to the innocent woman, there was a growing sense of anger that somebody could have been subjected to such an appalling attack. There was an overwhelming fear in the close-knit community and locals were keen that the individual responsible would be caught.

Gardaí quickly launched an investigation and 18-year-old Joseph Cummins, of St Joseph's Park, Nenagh, was arrested, within days of the attack. He was later charged with offences arising from the incident. In January 2007, Cummins, who was then aged 20, went on trial, accused of raping the woman, at the Central Criminal Court, sitting in Limerick. He pleaded not guilty to having unlawful intercourse with the woman and to anally raping her, in the early hours of 22 May 2005. He also denied threatening to kill her and stealing money from her home.

The victim sat through the trial with members of her family and gave evidence, during which she said her attacker warned her that she would never walk the streets again if she contacted gardaí.

Those present in the courtroom listened in stunned silence as the woman recalled waking up at 3.20 a.m. to take tablets. After hearing a noise in the kitchen, she went downstairs, where she was confronted by an intruder.

She said that she asked him to leave, but he came back in again through the back door, which she was unable to lock. She said he then pushed her on to an armchair and raped her twice. The woman, who lived alone, described how her assailant pulled her nightdress over her face while he raped her for 'what felt like about ten minutes. I kept asking him to stop, that he was hurting me. He said if I did not shut my mouth, he'd really hurt me.'

She said she tried to scream that she had a pain in her chest, but was told there was nothing wrong with her and that she was 'well able for it'. The intruder eventually left the house with her purse, which contained around €135, and warned her not to contact gardaí. The woman was very ill after he left her house and sat up until 8 a.m., before contacting her daughter to tell her about the horrific ordeal. When examined at the sexual assault unit at Waterford Regional Hospital, the victim had bruises to her neck and face.

The jury heard from Brendan Grehan, Senior Counsel for the State, who said that the question was whether the accused had perpetrated the alleged offences. While the victim had given gardaí a description of the intruder, she was unable to identify Cummins in an identity parade carried out at Nenagh Garda Station, after he was arrested. She had, however, given gardaí a detailed description of what the intruder had been wearing. Upon hearing this description, an eagle-eyed garda, Paul O'Driscoll, recalled seeing Cummins wearing the same clothes the previous day. Cummins was subsequently arrested and his clothes were seized during a search of his home.

A forensic scientist told the court that the victim's DNA was found on underwear belonging to the accused. This witness told the jury there was a one-in-600-million chance that DNA samples taken from the front area of his underpants would match anybody else's other than the complainant's. The witness also said that the chance of a DNA sample taken from a shirt belonging to him matching somebody other than the complainant's was one in a billion.

During the week-long trial, Mr Justice Paul Carney instructed the jury to find Cummins not guilty of threatening to kill the complainant. At the end of the trial, the jury of nine men and three women found Cummins guilty of raping and anally raping the woman, having deliberated for an hour and 40 minutes. He was also found guilty of burglary, at her home.

After the verdicts were brought in on 31 January 2007, the court was told that Cummins had 60 previous convictions —

despite his young age — and was on bail pending appeal when he committed the rape. On 20 May 2005 — just two days before the rape of the 74-year-old woman — he was jailed for 18 months at Nenagh District Court for road-traffic offences. However, he was granted bail pending an appeal to the Circuit Court. (An individual who receives a jail sentence in the District Court for a relatively minor offence is entitled to bail, if the sentence is appealed to a higher court. A recognisance is fixed by a judge and a bail bond is then signed by the individual lodging the appeal, before being remanded on bail.)

At Nenagh Circuit Court a year later, the sentence was upheld. Thirty-nine of Cummins' previous convictions related to road-traffic offences, including several for stealing cars. He also had convictions for assault (including an assault on a garda), criminal damage, theft and public order offences. However, he did not have any previous convictions for offences of a sexual nature.

The court was also told that Cummins had come to the attention of gardaí in Nenagh as a young boy. Mr Justice Carney complimented Nenagh gardaí on their work in the case and praised Garda O'Driscoll, who had seen Cummins wearing the same clothes described by the victim of the rape. The judge also paid tribute to Superintendent Catherine Keogh — who was based in Nenagh at the time — who led the investigation into what he described as an appalling outrage perpetrated on an elderly woman.

The judge declared Cummins a sex offender and remanded him in custody for sentencing in March 2007. Speaking after the guilty verdict was returned, the victim said she was relieved that it was finally over and said she was very happy with the jury's verdict.

The victim again attended court for Cummins' sentencing, at the Central Criminal Court in Dublin, on 12 March 2007. Mr Justice Carney handed down a 15-year sentence, after hearing the victim impact statement outlining the devastating consequences of Cummins' actions on the woman. The judge imposed two concurrent terms of 15 years for rape and anal rape and five years for burglary. The five-year sentence would run concurrently with the 15-year sentences. The 15-year term would start on the expiration of the 18-month sentence Cummins was serving at the time. The judge ordered that Cummins undergo ten years' post-release supervision.

When the woman's victim impact statement was read out, the court room fell silent as details of her frightful torment were outlined.

'I lived alone and was never afraid before that. It never really bothered me if the windows and doors were open during the day. I was surrounded by lovely people around the same age as myself. My neighbours were very good to me. If my smoke alarm went off, my neighbours would be straight over. I have great friends in the estate. The house was very easy to look after and I was close to everything. I used to love going down the town and meeting friends of mine and we used to go for a cup of tea.

'The reason my life suddenly changed completely was that on 22 May 2005, in the early hours of the morning, a man broke into my house where he raped me and robbed me in my living room. It was a vicious attack which has completely changed my life. I never felt afraid in my own house and I never thought anything like this would ever happen to me. Something like this should never happen to me or to anybody else. I was in poor health at the time. This incident seriously affected me in many ways. During this attack, I was terrified for my safety. Nothing like this has ever happened to me before. I never even had a reason to call the gardaí,' she continued.

'Not only has this affected me, it has affected my whole family. All our lives have been turned upside down. Shortly after the attack, we brought the armchair that I was raped in to my daughter's house. My daughters made up a life-size dummy and put it in the armchair. They then set fire to the armchair. I kept wishing that it was the man that did this to me was in the chair going up in flames.

'I am now terrified every moment of every day. I can't relax in my own home. I am terrified that someone is going to break in to my house again. I keep checking that the doors are locked, even though I know that they are. I keep hearing noises in the house and I ring my daughter to come in and check that everything is okay. I can't sleep at night and I am having terrible nightmares that he is going to come back again. The night this attack happened to me, I got sick in the sink. I cleaned up after myself.

'I had a box of sleeping tablets in my hand which I picked up from somewhere. I sat there thinking to myself would I be better off taking them and for my family to find me dead, rather than me having to tell them what had happened to me and for them having to go through all this,' said the woman.

The victim, who was 75 at the time of the trial and sentencing, moved from her home into accommodation beside one of her daughters, after the attack. Her family was extremely supportive of her and accompanied her to the trial every day, amid much emotion and heartbreak, as her unpleasant memories of her ordeal came flooding back.

'I don't leave the house any more now. I don't go down the town like I used to love doing because I'm afraid of meeting people. I don't go and visit friends any more, because I'm afraid to go out. I feel trapped in my house. I don't like where I'm living now because it's all young people that live there and I have no friends near me.

'I never told my family exactly what had happened to me on the night of the attack and they only heard the full details on the day I gave my evidence in court. That was very hard for both me and my family. All I want to do now is to put all this behind me, if I can, and put my life back together and live out the rest of my life as best I can,' the victim told the court.

Mr Justice Carney was told by members of the victim's family that when Cummins was being led out of court in Limerick after his conviction in January 2007, he turned to them saying, 'This is not over yet.' They said he then thumped the jury box as he passed it, while prison officers used an envelope to shield his eyes to stop him from staring at the victim and her family.

Mr Justice Carney said this threat by Cummins led him to consider imposing a life sentence. However, he said he would not impose a life sentence in view of Cummins' age, as that could mean he may find himself serving 55 years or more. By adding post-release supervision to a 15-year sentence, it would keep Cummins under control for 25 years.

The sentencing hearing heard details of Cummins' background. He had come from a disadvantaged background and, as a child, he had been diagnosed as suffering from Attention Deficit Hyperactivity Disorder (ADHD). He had dropped out of secondary school at the age of 14. His barrister said Cummins was 18 at the time of the offence and asked that he be given some light at the end of the tunnel.

Mr Justice Carney noted that Cummins had an appalling record, but that he had an absolute right to contest his trial, for which he could not be penalised. However, by so doing, he forfeited a right to the consideration given to people who pleaded guilty at an early stage. The judge said he sympathised with Cummins in relation to his dysfunctional background and the disorder from which he suffered.

Mr Justice Carney said it was not his normal practice to comment on garda investigations. However, he would comment on this occasion, because Cummins' crime had been cracked by what he described as 'old-fashioned bobby-on-the-beat' police work.

Cummins lodged an appeal against both the conviction and sentence, to the Court of Criminal Appeal and this was heard on 31 March 2008. The three-judge court refused the appeal, having heard details of all the grounds put forward by Cummins' lawyers. It ruled that there was adequate evidence on which the jury could have returned a guilty verdict.

His legal team based one of its grounds on the validity of a search warrant issued in respect of Cummins' home. The search warrant was issued to gardaí on 22 May 2005. It was sought pursuant to the provisions of the Criminal Justice (Miscellaneous) Provisions Act 1997 and in particular Section 10 of that Act. However, the printed search warrant contained an error. While it was headed correctly, in the body of the warrant, it authorised gardaí to enter certain premises on the basis that there were reasonable grounds for believing that evidence of or relating to 'an offence under the Sexual Offences Jurisdiction Act 1996' was to be found on those particular premises.

The Court of Criminal Appeal noted, 'The reference to the Act of 1996 is an incorrect reference and is accepted by both parties as being an incorrect reference and was admitted during the course of the trial as being an incorrect reference.' However, the court ruled that it was 'an error of form rather than an error of substance. That being so, the application for leave to appeal against conviction is refused,' ruled the Court of Criminal Appeal.

The court then turned its attention to the appeal against the sentence imposed on Cummins. It stated that it was a 'very, very serious offence committed against a person of 74 years of age' in her own home in the middle of the night. The court stated that citizens are entitled to feel secure within their own homes.

'The main argument which is made in relation to the sentence which was actually imposed is that it failed to have adequate regard to two factors and to a combination of those factors, that is, to the age of the accused and his rehabilitation, bearing in mind the principle that a sentence must be constructed having regard to the appropriate rehabilitation of the accused, and what might be called a combination of those, the peculiarity being that the applicant in the present case had just reached his majority,' noted the court.

It stated that there was no doubt that the age of a person should be taken into account and that the sentencing judge indicated that he had regard to the age of the defendant. The Court of Criminal Appeal stated that Cummins' lawyers had argued that the sentence imposed did not adequately take into account the question of age, 'but the court is not satisfied that this is so. The learned sentencing judge clearly had in mind, although certainly with some reluctance, the possibility of imposing a life sentence, or in the alternative, had regard for the age of the accused in the event that he were to impose a very lengthy sentence, but did not do so, taking into account the applicant's age, so that on the question of pure age, the court is satisfied that there has been no error in principle in respect of the sentence actually imposed or on the failure of the judge allegedly to have regard to age,' stated the court.

'On the question of rehabilitation, the court was faced with a certain amount of what might be called evidence not advantageous to the applicant. It is undoubtedly the case that the principle of rehabilitation is one of the pillars which a sentencing court must have regard to in constructing an appropriate sentence for the particular accused or convicted person. Ordinarily, one would find mitigating factors that could be taken into account that might lead to a sentence less than the sentence that was imposed in the present case. The applicant, as he was fully entitled to, maintained and continues to maintain his innocence and did not plead guilty and there is no obligation on him to do so. That is not a factor that can be taken into account by a sentencing judge in terms of aggravating factors.' The court went on to say that as this was the case, the reduction in sentence a person could expect if pleading guilty would not apply here.

The Court of Criminal Appeal stated that the offences were serious and the fact that they were committed by an individual who was on bail at the time was an aggravating factor.

'The learned sentencing judge appeared to take the view that these particular offences, and here the court confines itself to the sexual offences, were at the serious end of the scale and this court can find no basis for suggesting that they could be considered in any other light than as at the serious end of the scale, indeed at the very serious end of the scale. They were offences against a woman of 74 years of age, a widow who lived alone at the time . . . The offences certainly involved multiple serious degrading sexual events or assaults which the court considers would have justified, and did justify, the learned sentencing judge in placing them at the very serious end of the scale. They were combined with evidence concerning threats to the elderly lady and there was the aggravating factor which, according to the legislation, must be taken into account as being an aggravating factor, namely that the offences were committed while on bail.

'The court also has regard to the fact that the learned sentencing judge correctly took into account the victim impact statement and these all taken together are indicative of the fact that the learned sentencing judge did not err in any way in placing the events at the serious end of the scale,' stated the court.

The court also looked at the question of mitigating factors and pointed to Cummins' previous convictions, extending over a period of time. 'There does not appear to have been any evidence before the court which would suggest that opportunities given in respect of rehabilitation have in any way been taken into account or followed by the applicant, nor evidence to suggest that if further opportunities were given, these would have been in some way taken up or followed through. The evidence appears to be to the contrary, because there had been some application of a juvenile scheme, there had been sentences of a probationary nature and there had been an assessment from St Michael's in Finglas, and none of these appeared to have suggested in any way that the question of rehabilitation, even in respect of the attempts that had been given, had been or were likely to lead to any difference in respect of the matters in issue,' stated the court.

'The statement made by the learned sentencing judge that the applicant continued to be a constant risk to the community is, in the opinion of the court, a statement made with sufficient basis, if only in respect of the 60 previous convictions, and the absence of any indication that an opportunity would be taken by the applicant to change the position in which he found himself,' added the Court of Criminal Appeal, which refused leave to appeal.

———

Undoubtedly, the issue of crimes committed by people who are out on bail is extremely sensitive in offences of a sexual nature, particularly because of the severe impact on victims, many of whom never fully recover from their ordeals. In the wake of Cummins being jailed for 15 years, the executive director of Rape Crisis Network Ireland (RCNI), Fiona Neary, welcomed the sentence and described the rape of the woman as a 'particularly lethal crime'.

In December 2009, the RCNI published a report entitled *Rape and Justice in Ireland*. The report addressed the issue of bail and found that three-quarters of defendants were admitted to bail, usually conditionally, during the criminal justice process. The authors of the report recommended that no-one already convicted of rape should be granted bail on a fresh rape charge.

'Bail in rape cases should always be subject to strict conditions, which are swiftly and rigorously enforced. At a minimum, defendants should be required to be of good behaviour, to stay away from the complainant unless absolutely necessary and to stay within the jurisdiction of the Irish courts. Bail should not be granted to a defendant who has been convicted of rape,' stated the report.

The RCNI's legal policy director, Caroline Counihan, says the recommendations contained in *Rape and Justice in Ireland* are important, in terms of taking victims into account. 'We would very strongly support the recommendations. There should not be bail for persons convicted of rape. It's very distressing for survivors. In recent years, Fine Gael has drawn attention to it and there has been a dramatic increase in the number of people committing offences while on bail,' says Ms Counihan.

Figures obtained in May 2010 show that between January 2008 and March 2010, the chief suspect in each of 47 offences of a sexual nature was out on bail. According to Ms Counihan, this means that 47 victims were affected. 'Forty-seven cases. You'd wonder what criteria were used in those cases. One has to remember, the nature of sexual crime is really horrendous. In terms of its effect on victims, there is no such thing as a minor offence. Forty-seven might not seem a huge number, but that's forty-seven survivors,' she comments.

'I am concerned by the upward trend in the numbers of offences committed by people on bail, despite the change in law. There still seems to be an inordinate number of offences by people on bail. We have to ask the question, are the powers we have being used enough? That would be our concern. A remand in custody is not being sought or not being granted in a number of cases. It is now possible for the prosecution to ask for a remand in custody where there is a reasonable chance that offences could be committed. Are we using it enough? I don't know the answer,' says Ms Counihan.

One in Four, a support group for victims of abuse, believes there should be minimum mandatory sentences for serious sexual crimes. Maeve Lewis, Executive Director of One in Four, says reform is required in the area of sentencing. 'For the last twenty years, different groups have been campaigning for reforming the law in terms of rape and sexual assault. However, the courts have not changed and there is no coherent sentencing policy. It is almost down to a lottery on what judge you get. We believe that all judges working in the criminal courts should be trained [in the area of sentencing],' Ms Lewis told me.

'There is a lack of consistency in sentencing. The whole trial system needs to be looked at. The criminal justice system does not serve victims at all,' she adds.

The fact that Joseph Cummins was on bail when he raped the 74-year-old woman in Tipperary was of huge concern to support groups for victims of crime. According to One in Four, this is an area that needs to be addressed. 'The whole issue of bail and early release is problematic. Attention needs to be focused where people are in prison for very, very minor offences and those who are in jail for very serious offences. Everyone convicted of a sexual offence should be placed on the sex offenders' register and a post-supervision order should be imposed. That's down to the discretion of the judge. There needs to be consistency on that. The judicial system should liaise with the prison authorities in this regard,' says Ms Lewis.

Views on proposed changes to the bail laws vary and One in Four believes that certain changes are necessary. 'There is a constitutional issue here about the person's right to freedom. There need to be compelling reasons for someone to be in custody. Probation reports should be put in place here to assess if an alleged offender is at risk of reoffending, rather than depend on judges or legal practitioners.'

One in Four believes that rehabilitation programmes should be tailored to suit each individual convicted of offences of a sexual nature. 'The treatment programme for offenders has been completely overhauled and a new programme is in place.

A new up-to-date programme has been modelled on international research. It is a good programme, but it is voluntary and people can choose not to attend,' says Ms Lewis. She adds that those who opt to attend this programme should benefit in terms of early release from prison.

In the wake of Joseph Cummins being found guilty of raping the woman, Fine Gael immediately called for suspects who are granted bail to be tagged. The party's then Justice spokesman, Jim O'Keeffe, said the Cummins case underlined the need for electronic tagging of those granted bail.

'I was absolutely shocked when I heard about the case and I believe that it completely underlines the view taken by myself and Enda Kenny [the Fine Gael leader] that tagging should be introduced for those on bail,' he said at the time.

In February 2008, Fine Gael's then Justice spokesman, Charlie Flanagan, again stressed that electronic tagging should be used for those temporary release, after it was revealed that there were 272 prisoners on the 'missing list'. 'I was shocked to learn that 272 prisoners are currently at large. It is very disturbing for their victims and for all innocent civilians to know that these criminals, many of them dangerous, are on the loose. The number of missing prisoners completely undermines the system of temporary release for compassionate or medical reasons. There is an urgent need for a complete review of procedures for the temporary release of prisoners, particularly if we want temporary release to be available to prisoners in future. I support temporary and compassionate release, but we cannot tolerate a system where prisoners are able to go missing so easily,' he said.

In response to a query from deputy Flanagan on the issue in Dáil Éireann in March 2010, the then Minister for Justice, Equality and Law Reform, Dermot Ahern, said he was hopeful of bringing forward the legislation required to impose post-release electronic tagging of sex offenders.

'It is a complex area and, as the deputy knows, we have

existing legislation which would potentially allow tagging for sex offenders on temporary release. As Minister, I have been extremely reluctant to allow any sex offenders out on temporary release, whether tagged or not,' he said.

Chapter 10
The Scourge of Heroin

While cannabis is the most widely used drug in Ireland, those working in the area of drug abuse say heroin has the most profound impact. Heroin destroys lives and wreaks havoc on communities. Not only does its use have a major impact on addicts, but their families are also forced to bear the consequences and its impact on society is phenomenal.

The abuse of heroin has traditionally been largely confined to Dublin city, but this has changed dramatically over the years as virtually every pocket of the country — both urban and rural — has witnessed the effects of its abuse. It has become more easily available and its popularity has grown over time.

Medics have expressed concern that the surge in the abuse of heroin will place a burden on the health services in the country, as the fast rate at which people become addicted has resulted in lengthy waiting lists for treatment. In 2006, Merchants Quay Ireland stated that there were an estimated 14,452 heroin users in Ireland and more than 7,000 of those were engaged in methadone — used as a heroin-replacement drug to treat heroin addiction — treatment programmes, in an effort to free themselves of the drug. The organisation said that of all illegal drugs, heroin was the one associated with the greatest harm to individuals, communities and families. It expressed the view that problem heroin use has a serious impact on society and is associated with increased levels of crime and imprisonment and increased inequality and poverty.

———

Drug addicts would not develop their taste for heroin without the work of drug dealers, who ensure that supplies continue to filter through the community, despite anti-drug campaigns and garda crackdowns. Every year hundreds of drug-dealers are caught and jailed. While figures show that dozens of those are dealing while out on bail, this chapter will focus on one case in Cork and will also look at the figures relating to heroin — also known as diamorphine — use and its impact on society.

Somalia-born Abdulakim Yusuf was caught dealing heroin in Cork on several occasions. Yusuf was jailed for 11 years at Cork Circuit Court in June 2007, after a judge heard that he had been caught dealing the drug five times in a four-month period in Cork city. Yusuf, who had lived at various addresses in Cork, was under heavy garda surveillance at the time.

Yusuf pleaded guilty to five counts of possession of heroin for the purpose of sale or supply at a number of locations in Cork, between 23 September 2006 and 4 January 2007.

In the five times that Yusuf was caught at various flats in Cork city with heroin for sale or supply, the total quantity seized amounted to 76 grams. It had an approximate street value of €17,000. This represented between 30 and 35 per cent of heroin seized by gardaí in the city during this period.

Yusuf's home was first searched by gardaí on 23 September 2006. During the course of the search, pursuant to a search warrant, gardaí found five packages, each containing eleven individual packs of heroin. This amounted to 55 individual deals of heroin. The total weight of the heroin found was 6.5 grams, having a street value of €1,300.

Just over six weeks after the first offence, Yusuf was again searched by gardaí, on 6 November 2006. This followed a surveillance operation. Eleven individual packs of heroin were found concealed in his mouth. On the same date, a follow-up search of his flat was carried out. One deal of heroin was found and also a larger bag was found concealed in the flat. The total weight of heroin found was 26 grams, which had a street value of €5,200. As he had done in the first case, Yusuf made admissions to gardaí.

Then, on 11 November 2006, some five days after being granted bail in relation to the second offence, Yusuf's home was again searched by gardaí, who had obtained a search warrant. Gardaí entered the home and found Yusuf in the process of dividing heroin into individual deals. The total weight of heroin found on this occasion was 12.6 grams, which had a street value of €2,500. According to gardaí, he was co-operative and made full admissions. For this offence, he was sentenced to two years' imprisonment, which was consecutive to the three years he was handed for the first offence.

Yet, despite the close monitoring by gardaí, Yusuf continued to deal. His fourth offence was detected the following month. On 26 December 2006, gardaí again obtained a search warrant and searched his home. One package of heroin, weighing 10.5 grams and with a street value of €2,100, was found. Yusuf again made admissions to gardaí and was charged.

His final offence was detected by gardaí on 4 January 2007. On that occasion, gardaí searched his home, having obtained a search warrant. They found Yusuf in the process of cutting up and 'bagging' heroin. 133 individual deals of heroin were found. The total weight of heroin found was 20 grams, with a street value of €4,000. He admitted that he was selling the heroin and he was sentenced to three years in jail for this offence, consecutive to the three years for the offence of 26 December 2006.

In imposing sentence, on 27 June 2007, Judge Patrick J. Moran said he would make several of Yusuf's shorter sentences consecutive, to make an 11-year total, because Yusuf committed some of the offences while he was out on bail. The 11-year sentence would commence on 4 January 2007.

The judge said that the 32-year-old had shown a total disregard for the fact that he was under garda surveillance and he had continued to deal heroin despite the attentions of the gardaí. The court was told that Yusuf was addicted to heroin at the time, was ashamed of what he had done and that it was against his religion as a Muslim. Some time previously, he had lost his job as a forklift driver. His barrister asked the court to take into consideration that he had no family in Ireland.

Concerns over the growth in the use of heroin in Cork were raised during this court case. While the amounts seized were not huge, a garda said the increased use of the drug was a worry. Responding to a question from the judge in relation to the extent of the use of heroin in Cork, a garda said, 'Over the last three years, there has been an increase of use of heroin in the city. It is a worrying trend, especially from our perspective. The amounts are relatively small compared to other drugs, but it is increasing.'

The judge said that the sale of heroin in Cork was a worry and said that the city was fortunate that there had previously not been widespread availability of the drug. He said that this was the first case of possession of heroin for sale or supply that he had dealt with in court.

———

In the aftermath of Yusuf being handed an 11-year sentence at Cork Circuit Court, his legal team lodged an appeal with the Court of Criminal Appeal. The court took into consideration Section 10 of the Bail Act 1997, which stated that when the court is determining 'the sentence to be imposed on a person for an offence committed while he or she was on bail' and is required to impose two or more consecutive sentences, 'then, the fact that the offence was committed while the person was on bail shall be treated for the purpose of determining the sentence as an aggravating factor.'

In advance of making any decision on the appeal, the court looked at the background to the case. It noted that Yusuf had been found in possession of heroin on five separate occasions between 23 September 2006 and 4 January 2007, in Cork city, for the purpose of selling or otherwise supplying it to another.

'The applicant made admissions of these offences on each occasion and also admitted to being in possession of the same controlled drug, diamorphine [i.e. heroin], for his own use contrary to Section 3 and Section 27 (as amended by Section 6 of the Misuse of Drugs Act 1984) of the Misuse of Drugs Act 1977,' noted the court.

The submissions made by Yusuf's legal team were interesting, in terms of the issue of bail and in view of the fact that multiple offences had been committed. The three-judge Court of Criminal Appeal had to address carefully the issues raised by the applicant's legal team.

'It is submitted on behalf of the applicant that the imposition of cumulative consecutive sentences is wrong in law, that the wording of Section 11(1) does not require or mandate cumulative consecutive sentences,' stated the judges. The court looked at the argument put forward by Yusuf's lawyers and reduced the eleven years to nine. It ruled that only the three-year sentences imposed for the fourth and fifth offences (December 2006 and January 2007), should be treated as cumulatively consecutive to the three years for the first offence. The two-year sentence for the third offence (11 November 2006) should run concurrently with the sentences for the first and second offences. This would reduce the total period of imprisonment to nine years.

'It may be said at the outset that the imposition of consecutive sentences does not require statutory authorisation and is a well-established feature of Irish criminal law. That said, there is a strong tendency evident in the jurisprudence of this court to avoid the imposition of consecutive sentences where the offences might be described as falling within a similar pattern of offences or occurring within a relatively short timeframe. It could be said that those features are present in the instant case,' stated the three-judge court.

It also pointed out that if all the sentences handed down for offences committed by people on bail were consecutive, the results could mean lengthy sentencing. 'If every sentence to be imposed for offences committed while on bail had to be consecutive to any other sentence, the implications would be somewhat alarming. Where three or more such events occurred, the ultimate outcome might be a sentence of 20 or 30 years, or some other period of years which would be quite disproportionate having regard to the totality principle. Alternatively, the sentencing judge might have to fashion absurdly short consecutive sentences to ensure compliance with the totality principle.

'On the facts of the present case, the Court is of the view that to structure the sentence so that the sentence imposed for each of the last three sets of offences is made consecutive to each of the others did result in a total sentence which is disproportionately high, having regard to the relatively small amounts of drugs involved,' it ruled.

———

This case was remarkable for a number of reasons. It focused on drug-dealing in Cork; it highlighted the growth in the use of heroin and it also touched on the much-debated bail laws. The fact that the use of the dangerous drug heroin had significantly increased in the country's second largest city presented a major headache for the authorities. While this was attributed to numerous sources, the fact that one dealer, Abdulakim Yusuf, was on bail when he was committing offences was of huge concern, despite a heavy garda surveillance operation.

In July 2009, a joint policing committee in Cork heard that heroin seizures had increased 40-fold in the county over the previous four years. A senior garda officer told the Cork-City-Council committee meeting that the number of heroin seizures had increased from just four in 2004 to 159 in 2008. The meeting also heard that the number of people attending for treatment for heroin addiction in Cork had also increased significantly. More than 100 people attended for treatment both in 2007 and 2008, while there was a waiting list of more than 150 people at the time. The statistics were alarming.

The figures prompted fears that the escalation in the use of heroin in Cork would reach crisis levels within a few years. Worryingly, many of those using heroin were paying between €100 and €300 a day to feed their habit. Most addicts were using the drug on a daily basis.

According to official figures from An Garda Síochána, heroin accounted for 15 per cent of drugs seizures in Ireland in 2006. There were 1,115 seizures of heroin, which amounted to 128,097 grams. This was higher than the figure for ecstasy seizures, which accounted for 10 per cent of all seizures (771 cases). Cocaine was slightly higher than heroin, accounting for 18 per cent of all seizures (1,324 cases). However, cannabis remained the highest, in terms of the amount seized during 2006. Fifty-one per cent of drugs seized in Ireland involved cannabis (3,853 cases).

Garda figures also show that a significant amount of drugs offences are committed by people on bail. In 2005, 430 drugs offences were committed by those on bail, out of a total number of 5,456 headline offences committed by suspects who were out on bail at the time. During that year, the number of drugs offences in Ireland increased by 45 per cent; from 5,254 to 7,607.

Figures from the Central Statistics Office (CSO) show that between 2007 and 2009, thousands of drugs offences were committed by people who were believed to be out on bail at the time. There were significant numbers of cases of possession of drugs for the purpose of sale or supply. In 2007, there were 720 cases; in 2008, there were 891 cases, while in 2009, there were 713 cases. There was also a small number of cases of drugs importation, where the suspected offenders were on bail at the time. There were seven cases in 2007; four in 2008 and thirteen in 2009. There was also a small number of cases of cultivation or manufacture of drugs, where those believed to have been involved were on bail. In 2007, there were two cases; in 2008, there were five cases, while in 2009, there were three cases.

According to figures from the CSO, there has been a steady increase in the number of heroin seizures in Ireland between 2004 (612 seizures) and 2007 (1,698 seizures). The CSO figures also show that the number of proceedings for possession of heroin steadily increased each year between 2003 and 2006. In 2003, the figure was 995; in 2004, the figure was 1,201; in 2005, there were 1,601 cases and in 2006 there were 2,364 cases.

The growth in the use of drugs in Ireland over the past decade has been well documented and research has shown that the scourge of drugs has had a grave impact on society. Figures from the National Drug Treatment Reporting System (NDTRS) show that more than 14,000 people were treated for problem drug use in 2008. Of those, more than 6,500 had first entered treatment during that year. The report stated that the high number of people entering treatment was an indirect indicator of recent trends in problem drug use. Heroin showed up in the report, which stated, 'An opiate (mainly heroin) was the most common main problem drug reported by cases entering treatment.' Alcohol was reported as an additional problem substance in 41.4 per cent of all treated cases. The majority of cases treated in 2008 reported problem use of more than one substance (70 per cent), which was almost three per cent higher than the 2007 figure. Cannabis (40.7 per cent) and cocaine (36.8 per cent) were the two most common additional problem drugs reported in 2008.

———

The fight against the spread of drugs is a continuing one for gardaí, who believe that much of the heroin in circulation in Ireland originates in Afghanistan. In recent years, gardaí across the country have reiterated their concerns about the growing use of and dependency on heroin. They have pointed out that there is anxiety at the manner in which heroin has crept into society as the increase in the seizures of both heroin and cocaine is worrying. The increase in the number of seizures of heroin is due to a combination of factors, including additional garda resources to crack down on its use; the establishment of garda surveillance operations and the increased availability and use of the drug.

According to the An Garda Síochána three-year-review report 2006–2009: 'Garda resources in the fight against illicit drugs have increased. This is particularly evident with the creation of additional divisional and district drugs units. By the end of 2008, each division in the country had a dedicated drugs unit. The Garda National Drugs Unit and divisional and district drugs units are also supported in their work by officers from other national units, such as the National Bureau of Criminal Investigation, the Criminal Assets Bureau and the Garda Bureau of Fraud Investigation. The effective use of resources in the fight against illicit drugs is contingent on intelligence-led operations and An Garda Síochána collaborates with our colleagues in Customs and with international law-enforcement agencies. Our success to date is manifested in drugs seizures in excess of €880 million in the period 2006–2008.'

According to the Government's National Drugs Strategy 2009–2016, 'the volume of drugs seized has increased across almost all major drug categories, in particular cocaine and cannabis resin. While heroin seizures between 2000 and 2005 were relatively stable, there has been a significant increase in the volume seized in 2006 and 2007; and as well as the volume of seizures, the number of seizures conducted has increased by 59 per cent on 2000 figures, highlighting that the increased volumes are associated with an increase in the number of seizures and are not solely attributed to a low number of large seizures.' Among the strategy's priorities is to tackle the spread of heroin across the country, particularly in the major cities and in several towns.

In 2008, a government-supported campaign entitled, 'Dial To Stop Drug Dealing' was set up. It is an initiative aimed at tackling drug-dealing in local communities around the country. The information, collected anonymously, is passed on to gardaí. Dial to Stop Drug Dealing urges people to call a hotline and give information on drug dealing. Its establishment has led to several drugs seizures, after thousands of calls were made to the hotline by members of the public during its first year in operation.

———

Speaking at its annual review for 2008 in September 2009, Merchants Quay Ireland Chief Executive Officer Tony Geoghegan said that heroin abuse had become a national crisis. More than 5,000 drug users attended Merchants Quay Ireland's drug services in 2008. The report stated that heroin, in recent years, had become a major issue in many towns and cities across Ireland, many of which had previously been untouched by the problem. 'In 2008, we have seen an alarming increase in drug use outside of Dublin. Heroin respects no borders and users are now to be found in all areas from Ballyshannon to Ballydehob. Cities such as Cork and Waterford, that might have been considered relatively unscathed five years ago, now have significant problems. Heroin use is a national crisis. We now need a national network of crisis, treatment and family support services aimed at ensuring that help is available at the earliest possible opportunity, before problems become entrenched,' said Mr Geoghegan, at the time.

Now, a couple of years on, Mr Geoghegan doesn't believe the problem has been alleviated. He says that while the age profile of heroin addicts has increased from the 22–24 age bracket to the 28–30 mark, nevertheless, it is still widely abused. 'It is growing. You look at the prevalence estimates and it certainly has increased. Studies show there are approximately 20,000 heroin users now; which is a 6,000 increase on previous studies. The greatest growth is outside the greater Dublin area, in many of the urban centres like Cork, Limerick and Athlone. There have been significant increases in terms of the treatment of heroin users and in terms of arrests and seizures.

'Certainly there is an argument to be made that heroin use does flourish in areas of social and economic disadvantage, but I do believe that like people trying to get drug-free, they are starting from a lower base and find it difficult to get there [those in poor social backgrounds]. They wouldn't have the support that middle-class people have. There has been a big urbanisation all around the country. In all urban centres, there are pockets of disadvantage,' he explains.

'The gardaí have done a lot of work. It's difficult to evaluate their success if you use prosecutions as a yardstick. The biggest single prosecution is for possession. There is an argument to be made for another mechanism to deal with this, i.e. if someone is found with a small piece of cannabis on them, they plead guilty straight away and benefit from the Probation Act. It's a more efficient way. I think they need to look at more mechanisms like that. Having a conviction is a block to rehabilitation and reintegration,' he says.

Given the prevalence of drug offences committed by people on bail, several victims' groups have called for tougher bail laws to be introduced. However, speaking from his experience over the years, Mr Geoghegan believes that an individual's rights should be taken into account when it comes to bail.

'In the criminal justice system, you are innocent until proven guilty. Everyone is entitled to bail. If the police can make an argument that there is a likelihood to commit crime, I don't know how they can prove that. If someone is rearrested dealing while on bail, he is unlikely to get bail a second time. The usual procedure is if you breach your bail conditions, you are not likely to get bail again. The prison system is bursting at the seams,' he adds.

Heroin is always likely to be available in Ireland, but according to Mr Geoghegan, its likely impact on society is impossible to foresee. Cross-addiction has become more common as drug users focus on not just one, but a number of types of drugs, to feed their habits. 'It's hard to predict what sort of changes will come down the track. The profile of heroin hasn't changed a whole lot over the past five to ten years. Now it's a much more globalised industry. There are bigger gangs involved. That's the biggest change we have seen and I don't see many changes coming,' he says.

'The use in itself is a crime. In terms of petty crime like larceny, a high proportion of people who use heroin habitually get involved in crime to support their habit. There are two-way links. It moves the other way, too, in that some people would have been involved in crime before they got involved in drugs and the two overlap. It is not a one-way street.

'There is more poly drug use. You don't meet people just using one drug; particularly in small urban centres, people will use other substances. Cocaine is being used by a wider base. It has spread into sections of the population that wouldn't use heroin. It is more of a cool thing. While cocaine doesn't have the negative connotation that heroin would have, a lot of people who use heroin use cocaine as well. Cocaine is a stimulant and it can be hard to wind down off it. People would often use heroin to come down off that,' he tells me.

Looking to the recovery of heroin addicts, Mr Geoghegan believes that the criminal justice system can play a role in helping people to become heroin-free. A multi-pronged approach is desirable in any efforts to curtail the monumental problem. 'People do recover and move on. There aren't that many fifty-year-old and sixty-year-old heroin users around and that's because people do recover and can do very well. The criminal justice system can play a role in ordering treatment. There need to be better links between the criminal justice system and referring people to treatment but it comes down to resources. We only have fifteen residential detox beds in the country for the 18,000 to 20,000 heroin users. The State has placed an emphasis on the provision of methadone treatment to get people off drugs and we need to put an emphasis beyond that in supporting people to get drug-free.'

Chapter 11
Preying on the Elderly

The elderly are particularly vulnerable when it comes to crime. Many live alone, some a considerable distance from their families. Whilst they thrive on their independence, it can be quickly shattered. The experience or prospect of being targeted by criminals creates fear and anxiety for the older population. Although there are supports available through groups such as Neighbourhood Watch and Community Alert schemes, nevertheless the older population remains vulnerable and at risk.

In December 2009, a man who had broken into the homes of several pensioners in Dublin was jailed for eleven years. He committed some of the offences while he was out on bail. He was serving an eight-year term for other burglaries, but was granted early release. He had more than twenty previous convictions for similar offences.

That man was Anthony Connors, a drug addict, from Tulip Court, Darndale, Dublin. Arising out of the garda investigation into a spate of crime, in December 2009, Connors pleaded guilty to ten counts of burglary, three counts of false imprisonment, two counts of robbery, one count of assault and one count of handling stolen property. Connors struck in several parts of the city, including Dún Laoghaire, Donnybrook, Ranelagh, Ringsend, Blackrock and Phibsboro, between November 2007 and March 2008. Most of his victims were aged 70 and over and lived alone. He targeted people who were living in accommodation for the elderly. In most cases, he would call to the door and push past his victim, before ransacking the house. On some occasions, he would assault his victim, while on others, he would lock the victim into a bathroom or bedroom while he searched the house, before fleeing. Some of his victims were threatened with a knife or scissors and were dragged around their homes looking for money. Connors left a trail of havoc in his wake.

Dublin Circuit Court was told that the actions of the father-of-two — who was aged 34 at the time of sentencing, in December 2009 — had a profound effect on his victims. Many experienced nightmares and were fearful of leaving their homes. The court was told that one innocent, law-abiding man's final days were traumatic and stressful, after Connors had preyed on him. Connors had locked the 79-year-old man into the bedroom of his home and stole more than €500 from him. The man had died by the time the case came to court, due to a terminal illness, but Connors' actions had made his final months deeply upsetting. The victim told gardaí that he could not sleep and he did not feel safe in his own home, after what had happened to him.

On one occasion, Connors called to the home of a 67-year-old man. He held a knife to the man's throat and forced his way into the house. He told the man he was a drug addict and that he needed money. He took €750, locked the man in the bathroom and left the house.

On another occasion, Connors called to the home of a 68-year-old man. He said he was looking for the man's landlord's telephone number. The man told him he didn't have it and Connors forced him inside. He punched and kicked him as he lay on the ground and held a knife to his throat. He ransacked the house for money, before fleeing. Another victim, aged 73, was punched and kicked by Connors, after he forced his way into his home in Blackrock, Co. Dublin. He stole the man's medication and €260 in cash.

————

The victim impact statement of one of Connors' victims — an 81-year-old woman — explained how she was now living like a hermit after being targeted by Connors, who had forced his way into her home. She was afraid to open her door to anyone as a result of the torment inflicted on her by Connors, who stole more than €2,000 from her.

In court, through his barrister, Connors apologised to his victims. While Counsel accepted that the offences were disturbing, he said the defendant was remorseful. He said that Connors was a cocaine and heroin addict and had spent his childhood in institutions.

The sentences handed down to Connors ranged from six months to seven years. Some were consecutive, because those offences were committed while he was on bail. Judge Katherine Delahunt imposed jail terms totalling eleven years, with the final year suspended. She noted that the victim impact statements from those affected made difficult and tragic reading and said there was a distressing similarity to the crimes.

————

However, this was not the first time that Connors had come to the attention of gardaí for robbing the elderly in various parts of Dublin. In 2003, he pleaded guilty to nine counts of robbery at addresses in Dublin, along with one count of burglary and one of attempted burglary, on various dates in August and September 2001. At that stage, he had 15 previous convictions. He began the spate of robberies just two months after being released in June 2001 from a six-year sentence.

At Dublin Circuit Court, in 2003, he was jailed for eight years for robbing several elderly people in their homes. One of his victims was 100 years of age. In September 2001, he gained entry to her home after he broke a window. He lifted her from her bed and carried her around her home while searching for money. He took around £200, before leaving the house.

The day after this offence, Connors struck again. This time his victim was an 82-year-old man, who was living on his own. He stole £3,000 from the man's home and cut the telephone wires, before leaving the house. On another occasion — in August 2001 — Connors targeted a 69-year-old man. He knocked on the door of the man's apartment and requested a glass of water. He then produced a hammer and demanded money. The man was only able to give him £10. Connors then forced the man to walk about one kilometre with him to an ATM machine to withdraw more money. However, the man was unable to give Connors any further money as he only had £1 in his bank account.

Another of Connors' victims was a 78-year-old woman, living on her own in an old people's home. He pushed her into a chair and stole £200 from her. He also robbed a taxi driver and other elderly men and women of sums ranging between £6.50 and £360. A garda told the sentencing hearing at Dublin Circuit Court in June 2003 that Connors was arrested on 3 September 2001. He was released on bail and then committed three more crimes, before he was arrested again. His barrister also told that court hearing that Connors was extremely remorseful for his actions. The court heard Connors had a long history of psychiatric problems and was addicted to heroin.

Back in February 2000, Connors was jailed for six years, after Dublin Circuit Court heard that he stole cash from several pensioners while he posed as a worker with various charities.

Connors pleaded guilty to robbery and burglary at various old people's homes in the Clontarf and Whitehall areas on various dates in October 1998. He and a female accomplice posed as workers for Age Concern and other charities, and Dublin Corporation, and asked old people for money. They stole £110 and a pension book from an 88-year-old woman. They stole £15 from a 96-year-old invalid woman living alone, but Connors' accomplice gave £5 back to the woman before they fled. They also stole £215 and a credit card from a 66-year-old man at an old people's home in Dublin.

———

Connor's crimes had grave consequences for his vulnerable victims. The fact that several of the offences were committed while he was on bail highlighted a systems failure. Cases of this nature have opened up debates on the necessity to tighten up the bail laws and have led to calls for major changes to be implemented. To date, this has not been achieved.

Senior citizens have the right to enjoy their lives in peace and tranquillity and that right was robbed from them by Anthony Connors, who engaged in opportunistic crime. That even one senior citizen would be targeted in such a horrific manner is difficult to comprehend; the fact that Connors had so many victims is disturbing. He had continued on with his spate of crime, targeting one victim after another, before he was caught. He was eventually apprehended by gardaí, but by that stage, many lives had been badly damaged.

Victims of crime are upset by the actions of those who prey on them, but senior citizens are particularly vulnerable. Invariably, when older people speak out about crimes committed on them, they do not wish to be named, amid fears that they will be targeted again. Over the years, I have interviewed several older people who were victims of burglars. They suffer severe emotional trauma and nervousness afterwards and many of them are unable to stay at home alone after being burgled. They become petrified and feel that their independence has been stolen from them and their privacy invaded. They cannot relax until those responsible are taken off the streets and put into prison. Many of them bear the scars of their terrible ordeals for the rest of their lives.

Crime figures show that the number of burglaries committed in Ireland has consistently increased over the past decade. Burglars are keen to get their hands on valuables such as jewellery, cash, electrical goods and expensive household items. Sadly, burglars don't consider the consequences for their victims. In addition, burglaries account for a significant number of offences committed by people on bail. In 2007, there were 1,592 burglaries committed by offenders while on bail. This increased to 1,763 in 2008 and reduced slightly — to 1,677 — in 2009. In 2007, a total of 5,033 thefts were committed by those on bail. This increased to 6,023 in 2008 and decreased slightly, to 5,497, in 2009.

Older people targeted by burglars are angry and annoyed that they have been intruded upon. While they are relieved when those responsible for breaking into them are caught, they often feel that justice has not been done in that the sentences handed out in the courts are insufficient. When a defendant is fined or handed a jail sentence in the District Court, he or she is granted bail, pending an appeal to the Circuit Court. This is an individual's right, but, for the victim, it is almost unbearable. Not only do many of them find it difficult to understand the criminal justice system, but they also live in fear of being broken into a second time.

According to figures from the Central Statistics Office (cso), the number of burglary and related offences (which includes burglary, aggravated burglary and possession of an article with intent to burgle, steal or demand) increased by 9.4 per cent in the 12-month period ending 31 March 2010, when compared to the previous 12-month period. The figure increased from 24,395 (the 12-month period to 31 March 2009) to 26,680 (the 12-month period to 31 March 2010). There were 23,603 recorded burglaries in Ireland in 2007 and this increased to 24,684 in 2008. Given the difficulty of actually proving burglary offences, detection rates are low, but have risen consistently over the years. Detection rates were 17 per cent in 2004; rose to 18 per cent in 2005; further increased to 22 per cent in 2006; increased to 24 per cent in 2007 and again increased to 26 per cent in 2008. Relevant court proceedings commenced for 3,256 (13.2 per cent) burglary and related offences recorded in 2008. More than half (57 per cent) of those resulted in convictions. 16.9 per cent resulted in non-convictions, while 26.1 per cent of cases were pending when the statistics were compiled.

According to eircom PhoneWatch, burglary rates in Ireland have increased consistently over the years. According to its burglary report in 2008, burglaries increased significantly, by 32 per cent, between June 2007 and June 2008. During that time, €100 million worth of goods was stolen from homes. The figures showed that eight out of ten burglaries took place while home owners were at home. This was an increase on five out of ten, in 2004. 'The statistics strongly suggest that residents are not adequately securing their property while they are at home, and that burglars in turn are not deterred by home occupancy,' stated the report.

The statistics are shocking, but it is the trauma experienced by each and every victim that is most compelling. In 2008, The Commission for the Support of Victims of Crime stated that while the support of victims, particularly the elderly, can be met by the commitment of volunteers with a small amount of training, there was an increasing requirement for specialised training and specialised support. 'The degree of trauma is not measured by the seriousness of the crime, e.g. an elderly person who is burgled will often suffer life-changing effects,' it stated.

Age Action Ireland, a group that promotes positive ageing and better services for older people, says that older people should take safety precautions in their homes, to avoid being targeted by burglars. It also recommends that communities establish Neighbourhood Watch schemes. It encourages people to use door chains; to ask for photographic identification when answering the door and not to keep large sums of cash in their homes. Age Action focused on security in its pre-budget submission in 2009. 'The Irish Commission for Justice and Social Affairs argues that even for those who have never been subject to a violent assault, fear of violence can seriously undermine the quality of life. The cso found that 63 per cent of older people perceived crime as a serious problem in 2006. Since then the icjsa (2008) had found that the overall headline crime has increased eight per cent and Garda Síochána's crime statistics from February 2009 show a two per cent increase in theft and related offences, a four-and-a-half per cent increase in burglary and related offences. Increased crime levels and associated news reports will make older people experience fear of crime on a heightened level,' Age Action's report stated.

Those who manage Crime Victims Helpline, which provides support to victims of crime, say that older people living alone are vulnerable and can be easy targets for criminals. While most older people never experience a crime, for those who do, the experience is a very difficult one. Traditionally, people stored large sums of cash in their homes, rather than in financial institutions. Crime Victims Helpline urges older people not to keep money in their homes, as it can add to the potential risk of crime.

Retired judge Gillian Hussey is a patron of Crime Victims Helpline. Through her work over the years, she has seen the consequences of crime. While she has witnessed evidence of the pain suffered by victims of crime, she is also familiar with the various troubles experienced by many of those who commit crimes, several of who have been failed by society. She has seen conflicting emotions dominate cases that have been before her. 'A lot of these people are victims of society. I can see both sides,' she says.

'Everybody reacts differently to burglaries. If you have a family with a couple of children and their house is burgled, all of these people are very badly affected by burglaries. Being broken into is a huge thing for the elderly. It is a terrible invasion of privacy. Old people are very vulnerable, because unfortunately burglars tend to know what they are doing and they know their prey and they will go to somebody who is vulnerable. They [older people who have been burgled] are afraid they are going to be struck a second time. That is false thinking in most cases because if they are burgled the first time, the person who burgles them will have got what they want,' says Ms Hussey.

'A lot of it is opportunistic. A lot of them look and watch and they decide if somebody is living on their own. It is very difficult with older people. Most criminals seem to work in their locality. The ordinary decent criminals tend to stay in their own patches. They are lounging about. They know their victims. You can imagine the poor woman [victim] being traumatised. I don't know what you can do for her, other than being counselled. We have Community Alert. Some of the victims would be very unaware of little ways of security. They might look after themselves more diligently. We tend to get the panic alarm when we have been burgled.'

The entire courts process is difficult for every victim of crime, many of who find it difficult to understand its complex nature. Older people can find the entire process extremely overwhelming. Ms Hussey believes victims are forced to meet several barriers and expresses the view that victim impact statements should be more widely used in the courts. 'When an individual is granted bail before the case comes to court, the victim is traumatised. If he pleads guilty, she [the victim] may never hear what happened. In the other scenario, she is brought to court and she is in the same room as him. If he pleads guilty, that is the only time the victim gets an opportunity to have their say. In the District Court, you don't have a victim impact statement. You only have it in the Circuit Criminal Court and the Central Criminal Court. It is up to the judge to enquire if the victim wants to speak. I think something should be there. If somebody has been terrorised, it is up to the garda to bring him or her before the judge and explain how traumatised they are. If he pleads guilty, she is superfluous to requirements. Yet if he pleads not guilty and she's not there, she is the most important person in the courtroom. She has no rights. He has them all. The system is weighed very much in favour of the defendant. The system ignores victims,' she tells me.

During her time as a judge, she saw at first hand the excellent work done by gardaí in solving crime. However, she feels that very often victims of crime are quickly forgotten about, as time goes on. 'Most guards dealing with burglary cases are young. They don't understand the victim. The guard sees, "she said she was fine". He doesn't come back two or three weeks later to discover she is in bits and that there has been a delayed reaction. Victims don't understand the system. Nobody takes any time to explain the system to them. A burglary would be very low in the list of priorities for the court and the judge. If a judge was to put everybody in custody who had committed a burglary, then where would we go?' adds Ms Hussey.

Amidst spiralling rates of burglaries across the country, gardaí regularly express concern for the safety of the elderly. They issue warnings of the dangers of burglars and urge younger members of the community to look after their older neighbours. Neighbourhoods are actively encouraged to take part in programmes such as Community Alert and Neighbourhood Watch.

Established in 1985, Neighbourhood Watch is a crime-prevention and community-safety programme for urban areas. It operates as a partnership between An Garda Síochána and the public and encourages people to keep an eye on their neighbourhood. The scheme aims to help improve community safety, prevent crime and foster a caring environment for older and vulnerable people. The Community Alert programme has also been running for more than 20 years. It is intended to improve the quality of life of vulnerable people in rural communities, especially the elderly.

Both schemes are effective in that they ensure nobody is feeling alone and vulnerable, while there is a belief that public signage — indicating the presence of such initiatives in various localities — act as a deterrent for burglars.

However, it is not just the various agencies who are concerned about older people being targeted by burglars. The general public lists this as one of its key concerns. In January 2009, the then-Minister for Justice, Equality and Law Reform, Dermot Ahern announced the commencement of work on a project which will lead to a White Paper on Crime. The White Paper is due to be completed in 2011 and will set out the overall policy framework for strategies to combat and prevent crime. Numerous submissions have been made and various issues have been raised. Included among those is the need for protection for elderly and isolated members of the community.

According to the summary of the submissions made, 'There was particular concern for protection of the elderly, and the fear of crime felt by the elderly. Recommendations made with regard to the safety of the elderly included mandatory Garda presence in rural communities, Garda community liaison in community centres, Garda liaison with victim support at a local level, introduction of legislation to protect the elderly and include provision for senior protection officers in each Garda district and social workers tasked with elder abuse cases.'

'With this in mind, consultation has taken place on the first discussion document, "Crime Prevention and Community Safety". Interested parties were invited to make written submissions in response to the document and a series of five regional seminars were held in November and December 2009 with key stakeholders. The view was expressed among the submissions that information and education from gardaí on home security for the elderly was vital. 'Perhaps the gardaí could produce a leaflet on ways to improve home security. At the same time, there is a need to be sensitive to how this is explained as it may make older people living alone more nervous. It is important to give a sense of balance on this issue. The elderly are more vulnerable in society and are a special group. There is no legislation covering the elderly; in fact more protection of animals is afforded in law than of the elderly,' added the report.

In January 2010, Minister Ahern said that he was encouraged by reductions of crime in nine of the fourteen crime groups in 2009, compared with the previous year. However, he said he was concerned by the 2.2 per cent increase in property theft and particularly the fears of older people, many of whom live alone. 'Both the Garda Commissioner and I are concerned at the increase in property theft shown by the figures. Elderly people are subject to bogus callers to their homes. They must be vigilant, but likewise we must do what we can to protect them. I have met with the Attorney General with regard to the issue of mandatory sentencing for such crimes. He has requested the Law Reform Commission to examine the issue,' said the Minister.

Gardaí are, rightly, commended each time they solve a crime and prosecute a case. While society at large welcomes prosecutions and believes that victims are entitled to justice being done, those who work closely with the elderly do not believe there is faith within that community in the criminal justice system. A priest who works closely with the older population believes the system weighs in favour of the criminal and this leaves the victim exposed. 'It does. One hundred per cent. I've always believed it's a sign of a civilised society how we treat our children and our senior citizens and at the moment we are losing both. Our senior citizens are living in fear in so many of our communities and so many of them spend the night when they should be asleep, with the lights on, wondering when the dawn will come.'

Conclusion

As the eleven cases in this book demonstrate, the issue of crimes committed by those out on bail is not going to go away. The principle of a person being innocent until proven guilty is one of the cornerstones of our legal system and yet, as these eleven cases show, the crimes committed by those out on bail are often serious, with tragic consequences. Speaking on the subject of the 1997 Bail Act, during a debate in Dáil Éireann in 1997, the then Justice Minister Nora Owen (Fine Gael) explained that the country's bail laws had been of legitimate public concern for many years. She said that the introduction of changes in the bail laws was a priority and the Bill was one of the most important anti-crime measures introduced since the foundation of the State. 'This represents a fundamental rebalancing of our criminal justice system in favour of the victims of crime and the law-abiding members of society generally,' she told members of the Dáil, at the time.

'Up to now, many people received bail because only the fear of absconding or of interfering with witnesses could be used as reasons for refusing it. I want to send a loud message to those who commit crimes against people and property. Their crime days will be shortened by the use of this legislation which will prevent them from committing a series of crimes while on bail. Many criminals have boasted about the number of crimes — in some cases up to 20 — they committed while on bail. I hope those days are over,' added Ms Owen.

And yet, thirteen years on, serious crimes are still being committed by those on bail and there are still calls from political parties, NGOs and victims' rights groups for the bail laws to be strengthened. On the other hand, the Irish Council for Civil Liberties (ICCL) believes that victims' rights are deliverable without compromising the fundamental principles which lie at the heart of the criminal justice process: the right to a fair trial and the presumption of innocence. The ICCL believes that a fair and just criminal justice system should protect the human rights of defendants and victims alike. The ICCL monitors government policy on an ongoing basis to ensure that fair-trial rights are upheld.

In 2007, in a document entitled, 'What's Wrong With The Criminal Justice Bill 2007?' the ICCL stated that only anecdotal evidence has been produced to suggest that the current bail laws are ineffective. The ICCL recommends that the operation in practice of the current bail laws be independently reviewed, before action is taken to further restrict the right to bail.

The Irish Penal Reform Trust (IPRT)'s view is that individuals should only be remanded in custody where absolutely necessary. Its 'Position Paper on Penal Policy with Imprisonment as Last Resort' states, 'To significantly reduce the numbers of detainees on remand in Irish prisons, the criminal justice system should operate on the presumption of bail, and use remand into custody only where absolutely necessary. While we recognise that pre-trial detention may be necessary in some cases, the fact that remand prisoners are presumed to be innocent until proven otherwise at the trial means that detention should be used sparingly.

'The State should give consideration to the provision of bail hostels and bail addresses for those who are homeless or otherwise unable to reside at a specified address. Levels of financial sureties should also be reviewed to make sure that they are realistic, particularly in the current economic climate. IPRT also calls on the Government, the Courts Service and the Prison Service to conduct an analysis of how many people remanded in custody go on to receive a custodial sentence to assess the necessity of using this measure to the extent it is currently used,' it added.

The IPRT's Executive Director Liam Herrick accepted, in February 2010, that one common target of public concern was the problem of crimes committed on bail or while convicted offenders were otherwise at large 'and there is clearly a problem with some groups of persistent offenders racking up a long list of charges while awaiting trial'.

He said that while the 'knee-jerk reaction' was to make it more difficult to get bail — despite all of the associated problems of large-scale pre-trial detention — other methods could be found by probing deeper. 'A criminal justice system is about human behaviour and trying to change it. Reform of that system must be based on the best evidence of what individuals respond to, and it is practical issues such as court efficiency or bail supervision that promise better results than a forlorn hope that tougher sentences will have any beneficial effects,' said Mr Herrick.

It is not just the various groups and agencies and those directly affected by the bail laws who have an interest in seeing changes being initiated. In 2009, Dermot Ahern invited submissions on the White Paper on Crime, which, in 2011, will set out the overall policy framework for strategies to combat and prevent crime. As part of the consultation process, submissions were presented and the bail laws were the focus among some of those. It was argued, in some of the submissions, that the bail laws should be tightened and that bail should be refused in cases involving importing drugs, crimes using a weapon, armed robbery and repeat offenders. It was suggested that offenders on bail or remand should be required to surrender their passports.

While some families don't ever want to receive any information about the individual who inflicted trauma on them, others are keen to be updated on a regular basis from the Prison Service. A number of families who spoke to me during my research for this book expressed alarm that there is just one Prison Victim Liaison Officer for the entire country. They find it difficult to imagine that one individual is responsible for liaising with the many families who are facing troubling experiences, due to the effects of crimes committed. The Victim Liaison Officer is based at the Prison Service Headquarters and acts as the contact point for victims of offenders based in Irish prisons. According to the Prison Service, recent figures (June 2010) show that close to 150 families are availing of this service. 'The Victim Liaison Officer, when requested by a victim or victim's family, will make every attempt to inform them of significant developments in the management of the perpetrator's sentence as well as any impending release. Such significant developments could include temporary releases, Parole Board hearings, court or hospital appearances, prison transfers, expected release dates, etc.,' said a spokesman for the Prison Service.

'The Victim Liaison system places an onus on the victim or their family to make contact with the Victim Liaison Officer. When victims are ready, they can contact the service to say they wish to be informed in relation to significant developments in the sentence-management of an offender. When a prisoner is first convicted and sentenced to a term of imprisonment, the victim or the family in murder/manslaughter cases may not be ready at that stage to avail of the Victim Liaison service. They may wish to get on with recovering from their experience of crime or perhaps attend more to their grieving. For many victims, the last thing they want to think about, following sentencing, is the offender. The Irish Prison Service is fully aware that some victims/families may never wish to avail of the service, while others will do so when the time is right for them. Our primary concern is that victims and their families are treated in a sensitive, non-intrusive but informed way,' said the spokesman for the Prison Service.

The entire issue of Ireland's bail laws will, undoubtedly, rumble on. A decision to deprive an individual of his/her right to freedom is not taken lightly. Fair and balanced expert evidence should be presented before a judge, in every application to remand an individual in custody. The practice of granting temporary or early release to prisoners, specifically to manage the overcrowding issue, is not desirable and more prison spaces must be made available, if the criminal justice system is to be taken seriously. Many families of victims of crime feel let down by the system currently in place. They believe that a lack of consistency and a lack of information are twin evils, as they look for justice. A decision on whether bail should be granted or refused is at an individual judge's discretion and this process needs to become more consistent countrywide. Clearer guidelines should be made available to judges and these should be rigorously followed.

Relatives of victims of crime and the Irish public generally do not understand the different arms of the legal process, until they have been forcibly propelled into it for the first time, due to a particular crime visited on them. Although victim support groups and liaison gardaí work well with victims — despite limited resources — there is still a huge gap and a lack of understanding of each step of the process, particularly in relation to the bail issue. This also needs to be addressed.

It's impossible to wave a magic wand and find a workable solution to an issue which has spiralled upwards in recent years. However, one project which may be worth considering is 'Bail Support and Supervision Schemes'. Those schemes — which have been introduced in the UK — are designed to support and help individuals to attend court; to not reoffend while on bail and to abide by bail conditions. It would potentially remove several young people from the prison system and would also offer support programmes for them, while they are on bail. The goal is to keep them out of the prison system, thus reducing pressure on spaces. Currently, there is a lack of bail supervision in Ireland and there are insufficient deterrents for people not to re-offend. While the Probation Service — which is part of the Department of Justice — assesses and manages individuals after conviction, those granted bail in advance of trial or sentence are largely unsupported. A Bail Supervision Scheme would provide support that is essential in an effort to prevent re-offending, in many cases. In the face of severe pressure on the prison system and an increase in crimes committed by people on bail, it is a scheme that could benefit society as a whole. While additional resources would have to be pumped into it, the overall benefits would potentially be very significant. A new Bail Bill is currently being proposed — the purpose of which is to consolidate and update bail laws, in an effort to ensure that the bail regime can operate in as tight and effective a way as possible — but unless the necessary resources are made available, legislation will not meet public needs or allay public fears.